Instructional Illusions

Paul A. Kirschner
Carl Hendrick
Jim Heal

Together we unlock every learner's unique potential

At Hachette Learning (formerly Hodder Education), there's one thing we're certain about. No two students learn the same way. That's why our approach to teaching begins by recognising the needs of individuals first.

Our mission is to allow every learner to fulfil their unique potential by empowering those who teach them. From our expert teaching and learning resources to our digital educational tools that make learning easier and more accessible for all, we provide solutions designed to maximise the impact of learning for every teacher, parent and student.

Aligned to our parent company, Hachette Livre, founded in 1826, we pride ourselves on being a learning solutions provider with a global footprint.

www.hachettelearning.com

Although every effort has been made to ensure that website addresses are correct at time of going to press, Hachette Learning cannot be held responsible for the content of any website mentioned in this book. It is sometimes possible to find a relocated web page by typing in the address of the home page for a website in the URL window of your browser.

Hachette UK's policy is to use papers that are natural, renewable and recyclable products and made from wood grown in well-managed forests and other controlled sources. The logging and manufacturing processes are expected to conform to the environmental regulations of the country of origin.

To order, please visit www.HachetteLearning.com or contact Customer Service at education@hachette.co.uk / +44 (0)1235 827827.

ISBN: 978 1 0360 0891 8

© Paul A. Kirschner, Carl Hendrick, and Jim Heal 2025

First published in 2025 by
Hachette Learning,
An Hachette UK Company
Carmelite House
50 Victoria Embankment
London EC4Y 0DZ
www.HachetteLearning.com

The authorised representative in the EEA is Hachette Ireland, 8 Castlecourt Centre, Dublin 15, D15 XTP3, Ireland (email: info@hbgi.ie)

Impression number   10 9 8 7 6 5 4 3 2 1
Year   2029 2028 2027 2026 2025

All rights reserved. Apart from any use permitted under UK copyright law, no part of this publication may be reproduced or transmitted in any form or by any means, electronic or mechanical, including photocopying and recording, or held within any information storage and retrieval system, without permission in writing from the publisher or under licence from the Copyright Licensing Agency Limited. Further details of such licences (for reprographic reproduction) may be obtained from the Copyright Licensing Agency Limited, www.cla.co.uk

Illustrations by DC Graphic Design Limited, Hextable, Kent.
Typeset in the UK.
Printed in the UK.
A catalogue record for this title is available from the British Library.

Endorsements

'*Instructional Illusions* is a tremendously timely book that forensically takes apart many of the most persistent misconceptions in education today. In particular, the section on the Performance Illusion shows how the superficially plausible belief that assessments performance equates deep understanding is responsible for so much bad practice. In an age where AI can easily complete assessments, this corrective has never been more important. This is a must-read for teachers and leaders concerned with improving student learning in lasting ways.'

Daisy Christodoulou, Director of Education, No More Marking

'One of the greatest challenges of learning goes mostly unseen; we *think* we can tell when we (or others) are learning, but our perceptions are often wrong. This excellent, brief volume exposes the most common and pernicious of these errors, and describes how to correct them. Educators, parents, and students… get ready to be shocked, and then to learn!'

Daniel T. Willingham, Professor of Psychology, University of Virginia and author of *Why Don't Students Like School?*

'*Instructional Illusions* by Paul Kirschner, Carl Hendrick, and Jim Heal is an entertaining and insightful antidote to many insidious misconceptions about how learning and instruction work that are currently infecting educational practice. If you are interested in how an evidence-based approach can improve education, this little volume belongs on your bookshelf.'

Richard E. Mayer, Distinguished Professor of Psychological and Brain Sciences, University of California, Santa Barbara

'A major purpose of all science is to free us from illusions. Ou r senses tell us the earth is flat, but science disabuses us of that illusion. The science of learning equally disabuses us of educational illusions, but we have not had a compendium that indicates the illusions and their correctives. Now we have such a compendium providing a historical marker indicating where we have been and where we are now. Given the previous work by these authors, we might expect a superbly written book. And that is exactly what we have.'

John Sweller, Emeritus Professor of Educational Psychology, University of New South Wales

'This book is a boon for educators and students. The authors describe and illustrate conceptual roadblocks in teaching and learning that must be overcome to be successful. The illusions they describe so well are common ones that hinder education, and their recommendations for overcoming them will help learners and teachers. I highly recommend this book.'

Henry L. Roediger III, James S. McDonnell Distinguished University Professor, Washington University, co-author of *Make It Stick: The Science of Successful Learning*

'Teaching is perhaps the best known and least known profession. Since we have all been taught at some point in our lives, we presume to understand it. Having seen absurd portrayals in popular culture, we are inclined to think of it in terms of simplistic caricature. And knowing that it has been around for roughly time immemorial we tend to believe it consists of processes that can be understood by simple, sensible observation alone. None of this is true, of course, and the resulting misconceptions come at massive cost to students and society. At last, in the hands of Kirschner, Hendrick, and Heal, the most persistent illusions about classroom and cognition are ably and clearly laid to rest, replaced with a clear model of how learning works. Their book is a gift to educators (and those they educate) and should be on every teacher's bookshelf.'

Doug Lemov, author of *Teach Like a Champion*

Instructional Illusions is a remarkable book that fuses scholarly depth with classroom practicality. Far more than a critique of educational fads, it celebrates the science of learning by making visible the core issues that truly drive student growth. With clarity, compelling stories, and humility, the authors lift the veil on deeply embedded misconceptions and guide us toward practices that have real impact. This is a gift to anyone serious about improving teaching and learning.'

John Hattie, Melbourne Laureate Professor Emeritus

'Anyone involved in education will find this book invaluable! Kirschner, Hendrick, and Heal show us how cognitive biases can undermine effective teaching, and they offer clear, evidence-based strategies to recognize and overcome these instructional illusions. Grounded in the science of learning, this book is filled with practical examples and actionable advice. It's also a great read!'

Anna Stokke, Professor of Mathematics, Winnipeg University

'*Instructional Illusions* is an important must-read for teachers, students, and parents. It offers practical, immediately useful information backed by first-rate, contemporary scholarship. It not only highlights common illusions experienced by students and educators but also explains that these illusions are perfectly normal and offers actionable solutions to "unmask" the illusions. It is an incredible achievement to distill cutting-edge research on the science of learning into practical recommendations and a brief, accessible format.'

Jeffrey D. Karpicke, James V. Bradley Professor of Psychological Sciences, Purdue University

About the authors

Paul A. Kirschner is emeritus professor of educational psychology at the Open University of the Netherlands, guest professor at the Thomas More University of Applied Sciences in Belgium, and owner of kirschner-ED. He is a research fellow of the American Educational Research Association, the International Society of the Learning Sciences, and the Netherlands Institute for Advanced Study in the Humanities and Social Science. He holds an honorary doctorate (doctor honoris causa) from Oulu University in Finland. His most recent books are *How Learning Happens* and *How Teaching Happens*.

Carl Hendrick holds a PhD in education from King's College London and has taught for several years in both the state and independent sectors. He is currently a professor of evidence-informed learning and teaching at Academica University of Applied Sciences with a focus on bridging the gap between research and practice. He is co-author of *What Does This Look Like in the Classroom?*, *How Learning Happens*, and *How Teaching Happens*.

Jim Heal is professor of evidence-informed educational leadership at Academica University of Applied Sciences. Prior to that, he worked at Deans for Impact, a US-based non-profit infusing the science of learning into educator preparation, and at Harvard's Research Schools International initiative. He earned his doctorate in educational leadership from the Harvard Graduate School of Education and is author of *How Teaching Happens* and *Mental Models: How Understanding the Mind Can Transform the Way You Work and Learn*.

About the authors

Dedication

Writing this book has been a difficult collaborative effort – one that was shaped from the onset by the insights and scholarship of Prof. Dr Piet van der Ploeg. Piet's early contributions were instrumental in forming and refining the ideas that form the book's foundation, and his influence can be felt throughout the book.

As a scholar of educational philosophy and ethics, Piet spent his career exploring difficult foundational questions such as: what's the purpose of schooling? How should we balance transmitting knowledge with cultivating independent thought? What role does education play in shaping citizenship and democracy? Difficult questions with complicated answers.

Anyone who has had the privilege of working with Piet knows that he brings a rare combination of intellectual rigour, humility, and deep commitment to everything he does. He has a way of asking the kinds of questions that challenge your assumptions, sharpen your arguments, and push your ideas to a higher level. His reflections on citizenship education, pedagogy, and the role of research in teaching practice have profoundly shaped our own thinking, and we don't doubt for a second that his work will continue to inspire educators and researchers for years to come.

Though he was unable to continue as a co-author and work on this book, his presence in this book can be felt. Many of the discussions here were shaped by conversations we had, by his thoughtful critiques, and by the spirit of inquiry and reflection that he so strongly represents. It's impossible to write about evidence-informed teaching without acknowledging the impact of his work, and we hope that in some way, this book reflects the depth of thought and dedication that he has always brought to the field.

For his friendship, his wisdom, and his generosity of thought, we are truly grateful.

To my grandchildren, who teach their (grand)parents well. – *Paul*

To my father, for a lifetime of patient instruction. – *Carl*

To my dad. Thank you for being my first and best teacher. – *Jim*

'The world is an illusion, but it is an illusion
which we must take seriously.'
Aldous Huxley

'We are such stuff as dreams are made on,
and our little life is rounded with a sleep.'
The Tempest, **Act IV, Scene I**

'What the eyes see and the ears hear, the mind believes.'
Harry Houdini

Contents

Foreword: Dylan Wiliam 1

Foreword: Robert and Elizabeth Bjork 5

Introduction 7

1. The engagement illusion 15

2. The expertise illusion 21

3. The student-centred illusion 29

4. The transfer illusion 37

5. The easy-wins illusion 45

6. The motivation illusion 51

7. The discovery illusion 59

8. The uniqueness illusion 65

9. The performance illusion 71

10. The innovation illusion 79

Conclusion 87

Endnotes 89

Foreword

In the 1980s, I was involved in redesigning a teacher education programme, and one of the things we did as part of that work was asking students on the existing course which aspects of their studies were helpful and which were not. The answers we got were fairly predictable – students found practical teaching experiences in schools hugely valuable but were critical of many of the college-based courses they were required to complete, especially those that were not focused on the subjects they were teaching.

These college-based courses covered issues such as the philosophy, psychology, and sociology of education, and while these are undoubtedly important – especially if educators are to be professionals rather than technicians – our student teachers clearly had difficulty seeing the relevance of these courses to the practicalities of teaching.

Part of the problem was one of timescales. At the time, there was little systematic in-service professional development, and few teachers undertook formal study beyond the initial teaching qualification, so there was pressure to include everything teachers would need for their whole career. But the bigger problem was one of focus; put bluntly, the students found it difficult to see the relevance of the content of the so-called foundation disciplines to their immediate priorities – managing classroom teaching in schools.

In a sense, the teachers had a point. The work of Piaget and Vygotsky did not provide concrete evidence about what to do in classrooms. Piaget's work on developmental stages was often taken to mean that material that teachers were required teach was somehow 'developmentally inappropriate', despite important texts like Margaret Donaldson's *Children's Minds* showing how far children's actual capabilities diverged from what their development stage said they 'should' be able to do. And Vygotsky's careful distinction between learning and development was often completely ignored, so that teaching in the 'zone of proximal development' amounted to little more than teaching things the students did not know yet – hardly a deep insight.

This was all the more unfortunate because key texts such as Robert Gagné's *The Conditions of Learning* (1965) and David Ausubel's *Educational Psychology: A Cognitive View* (1968) provided clear advice to teachers about how to design effective instruction – advice that still stands up well today.

Why these timeless texts did not feature more prominently in teacher preparation programmes is obviously a complex issue, but it seems to me that a major factor was the perception that engaging with these texts was not only challenging, requiring careful analysis of the material to be taught, but that it was also not even necessary, as many students seemed to learn through exploration and play.

It is easy to see how such a belief might arise. For example, many children seem to learn to read effortlessly. Work by Robert Pianta and his colleagues shows that for approximately 25% of students, progress in early reading is independent of the quality of instruction they receive (Pianta et al., 2008), so if it works for these students, surely it should work for all. However, we now know that this is simply untrue. As Catherine Snow and Connie Juel conclude in their summary of early reading instruction, 'Attention to small units in early reading instruction is helpful for all children, harmful for none, and crucial for some' (Snow and Juel, 2005, p. 518).

In a similar vein, many children just 'get' mathematics, so why not emphasise playful exploration rather than formal teaching? The answer is, of course, that while it may work for some children, it will be a disaster for others, leading to huge variations in achievement, with many students becoming convinced that they can't learn.

Fortunately, over the last few decades, there has been a huge increase in the number of high-quality guides that demonstrate how cognitive psychology can be applied to make teaching effective. Unfortunately, there is so much out there, that it can be overwhelming.

This is why this book by Paul, Carl, and Jim is such an important contribution to the literature on effective teaching. First, it is short, which is important since I now believe that opportunity cost is the most important idea in educational improvement – any hour that a teacher spends on one thing is an hour they don't have to spend on something else. Second, it is authoritative; the authors are experts in the relevant research, knowing the key findings, but also aware of the limitations of the studies they discuss. Third, and perhaps most important, the book is practical, with implications for classroom practice drawn out in every chapter. Anyone interested in making teaching more effective should read this book.

Dylan Wiliam, Emeritus Professor of Educational Assessment, UCL Institute of Education

References

Pianta, R. C., Belsky, J., Vandergrift, N., Houts, R., & Morrison, F. J. (2008). Classroom effects on children's achievement trajectories in elementary school. *American Educational Research Journal*, 45(2), 365–397.

Snow, C. E., & Juel, C. (2005). Teaching children to read: What do we know about how to do it? In M. J. Snowling and C. Hulme (Eds.), *The science of reading: A handbook* (pp. 501–520). Wiley.

Foreword

This is a quite remarkable book, one that is unique in how effectively it blends cognitive science research, mostly carried out in the laboratory, with classroom research. This book is also remarkable from a historical standpoint, given the linkages it provides to the insights of educators, researchers, and philosophers tracing back to Aristotle.

To say that we admire what the best of K–12 teachers accomplish is an understatement. We have spent our careers teaching students who have already succeeded in acquiring knowledge and learning skills – that is, undergraduate students, graduate students, and postdoctoral fellows – who, prior to any contributions on our part, bring not only a foundation of prior learning, but also the skills, habits, and values that contribute so heavily to new learning.

At all levels of education, though, even at the college level, a fundamental fact is that any new learning builds on old learning. As the authors emphasise, learners at any level 'come to understand new information by reference to what they already know', and that they will activate that prior knowledge during new learning 'even if that knowledge happens to be incomplete or inaccurate'. From that perspective, what the best of teachers accomplish when teaching a class of, say, 20–30 students, each of whom brings some level of accurate, inaccurate, or incomplete knowledge, is quite extraordinary.

Yet another challenge teachers confront, though, as the authors emphasise, is assessing whether a given student has achieved the level of understanding and integration of new knowledge with relevant prior knowledge such that the new knowledge will transfer to the real-world contexts and/or subsequent classroom learning where it is relevant. Information and procedures that can be readily accessed in the teaching context can become inaccessible in some real-world contexts where they are needed.

The primary goal of instruction, then, is to facilitate students' long-term learning – that is, to create relatively permanent changes in comprehension, understanding, and skills of the types that will support long-term retention and transfer. During the instruction or training process, however, knowing whether such learning has been achieved is a challenge. What we can observe and measure is *performance*, which is often an unreliable index of whether the relatively long-term changes that constitute *learning* – as measured at a later time and place – have taken place.

Among the many strengths of this book, which makes it especially valuable in our view, is that the authors provide a theoretical rationale as well as empirical evidence for the instructional innovations they advocate. We are biased, of course, because that theoretical framework has emerged from, and been a guide to, our own research and teaching.

Robert A. Bjork and Elizabeth L. Bjork, Professors Emeriti, University of California, Los Angeles

Introduction

As far as we know, the earliest known illusionist was Dedi of Djed-Sneferu, a fictional ancient Egyptian magician appearing in a story told in the legendary *Westcar Papyrus*.[1] According to that text, Dedi's most renowned trick involved decapitating a bird before miraculously restoring it to life. Like all the illusionists who have followed, Dedi's trick worked not because of the initial act of disappearance (or in this case, decapitation). Rather, it relied on his ability to bring that missing something back from the brink. This step is critical to any illusion since it turns our attention away from the trick and towards ourselves – for in that moment, we acknowledge the illusory nature of our reality.

In their fascinating book *Sleights of Mind: What the neuroscience of magic reveals about our everyday deceptions*,[2] neuroscientists Stephen Macknik, Susana Martinez-Conde, and Sandra Blakeslee explore how magic reveals deep truths about the everyday cognitive deceptions that pervade our lives. Among the many points of confluence between magic and the mind, the authors explore how our brains interpret and 'make up' the world based on limited informational input, how attention is a scarce resource that illusionists can use to their advantage, and how memory is so unreliable that our recollections of events are prone to manipulation. In other words, illusions only work because humans are cognitively predisposed to being deceived.

In this sense, every walk of life has the potential to deceive us – yet few professions are implicated by the dissembling power of illusion more than education. After all, so much of what occurs when we learn is obscured to the outside observer, and often what we think we are seeing is distant or even diametrically opposed to what's really happening.

Instructional illusions take many forms and can make certain approaches to learning appear more effective than they really are. We see this when students seem engaged in a task but the activities they are working on have no relation to the intended aims of the lesson; or whenever students perform well on a test and we assume that they have learned that content in deep, durable ways that can be transferred to other contexts. These phenomena have been referred to by Professor Robert Coe as 'poor proxies for learning',[3] but it would be just as accurate to describe them as instructional illusions in the purest sense.

Conversely, instructional illusions mean we also overlook or undervalue aspects of teaching and learning that are more effective than they might first seem. We experience this whenever we mischaracterise excellent teaching as a 'knack' rather than the product of knowledge and finely honed techniques, or whenever we see students struggling with the complex nature of an idea and assume learning is not happening within that struggle.

Like many illusions or mass deceptions (such as conspiracy theories and the like), there is often a grain of truth in what we believe works. For instance, knowing that children learn to walk and talk without structured support can mistakenly lead one to believe that the process of learning to read will be similarly innate.

In short, teaching and learning can feel like a hall of mirrors in which nothing is ever quite what it seems. This is where this book comes in.

Across its chapters, we 'lift the curtain' on ten educational illusions to demonstrate how the surface phenomena of teaching don't tell the whole story. With reference to evidence from the world of cognitive science and educational psychology, we show that understanding how learning occurs can give us the eyes to see what lies beneath.

Common illusions about teachers, teaching, and learning

Teaching is not a straightforward process but rather a multifaceted endeavour, the complexity of which is dizzying to comprehend – *if* one decides to look closely enough. In professions like medicine, law, or engineering, we rightly assume there is more to know than what appears on the surface. Yet, when it comes to education, the fact that we have all *been taught* at some point in our lives bestows a false assurance in our understanding of teaching and learning. This misplaced confidence means we tend to brush over the deeply nuanced characteristics of instruction in favour of more convenient definitions.

We need only look at media portrayals of education to see this at play. Take the film *Dead Poets Society*, where Robin Williams plays John Keating, a passionate, idealistic English teacher at an exclusive all-boys' private school. Here, we find embodied all the idealistic, inspirational qualities of a teacher who leaves a lasting impact on his students. Unconventional in his methods, Keating empowers his students to find their own voices as they recite poetry and gaze longingly into the mid-distance. A classic portrayal of a thespian constructivist. At the other end of the spectrum is the authoritarian Mr Vernon in the movie *The Breakfast Club*. Mr Vernon, by contrast, enforces strict discipline, expects complete obedience with severe consequences for any rule violation, lacks empathy and understanding for what students are going through, belittles his students' concerns and opinions, and is generally cold and unfeeling when it comes to their wellbeing. A classic portrayal of the cold-hearted instructivist.

This caricaturing is not lost on Larry Cuban, who notes how teachers in popular culture are portrayed either as a 'clueless wag', an 'inappropriate role model', or a 'saintly sage who unlocks the hidden creativity of their students or rescues downtrodden minority children'.[4] The reality is that such depictions rely on crude stereotypes and oversimplified narratives that perpetuate the illusions of what teachers do.

Lastly comes the dissembling nature of the polarised political and policy debates about education and the role it ought to play in society. Political discourse about education often oversimplifies complex issues and distils the challenges that teachers face into plausible soundbites and straightforward solutions. They perpetuate the false idea that teachers alone can solve all educational and societal challenges despite the obstacles that politics and policy throw in their way. What remains is a system where initiatives that *seem* promising for students and learning can pass muster without being held accountable to evidence.

And so, when faced with incomplete and often inaccurate depictions of teaching and learning, we do what any pattern-seeking primates would do: we fill in the blanks, connect dots that don't exist, and seek answers to questions that haven't even been asked – all of which are optimal conditions for mass illusion to take hold.

Here are just a few of the misconceptions about teaching that have been afforded misplaced credence for so long:

- **Anyone can teach:** Teaching is often viewed as a fallback career, with the assumption that anyone who knows a subject can teach it. However, effective teaching requires a unique set of skills, including the ability to communicate complex ideas clearly, manage a classroom, engage students, and adapt to diverse learning needs.

- **Teaching is a job, not a profession:** Teaching is sometimes viewed as a lesser career compared to other professions like medicine or law. However, teaching is a complex profession requiring specialised training, ongoing education, and a commitment to ethical standards and continuous improvement.

- **Teaching is a calling, not work:** There's a common feeling that all teachers are highly idealistic about what they do and would even do it for free if that was necessary. They do all of the 'extra' unpaid work going as far as paying for school materials that the school doesn't provide out of their own pockets. However, teaching is a profession where teachers expect to be paid according to their training and investment of time.

- **Teachers work short days and have summers off:** While it may appear that teachers have short work days and long summer vacations, most if not all spend many additional invisible hours planning lessons, grading assignments, meeting with parents, proctoring school activities, participating in professional development, and so forth. Summers are often used for curriculum planning, classroom organisation, and further learning.

- **Teaching is easy:** Every adult should be able to manage a group of kids. All we can say is try managing 25-30 children from differing backgrounds with different needs. Teaching is incredibly challenging. It requires managing diverse groups of students, each with their unique learning and societal needs and backgrounds. Teachers must also navigate administrative tasks, changing curricula, and accountability measures, all while fostering a positive learning environment.

- **Good teaching is all about fun:** While fun and engaging lessons are important, effective teaching involves discipline, structure, and sometimes even rote learning (please excuse our French). Balance is key, as students need to build foundational skills that may not always be 'fun' to learn.

- **Teachers just need to know their subject:** Subject matter expertise is important, but it's only one part of teaching. Pedagogical knowledge – the understanding of how to teach – is equally crucial. Good teachers need to know how to present material in accessible ways, assess understanding, and adapt their teaching to different learning needs.

- **Just knowing how to teach is enough:** There is a misconception that if a person has mastered the 'tricks' of the teaching trade and can implement them, the subject matter isn't really necessary, and that you only need to be one lesson ahead of the students to be a good teacher. However, research (see endnote 12) has shown that excellent teachers have a deep conceptual knowledge of both how children learn and the subject they teach.

- **The teacher's main job is to impart knowledge:** Modern education focuses not only on content knowledge but also on developing skills like critical thinking, problem solving, collaboration, and adaptability once the content knowledge and skills have been mastered (see endnote 11). Teachers also play a crucial role in guiding students to become independent learners; teaching them how to learn.

- **Teaching hasn't changed much over time:** The trope is: take someone born 100 years ago, place them anywhere in today's world and they will be amazed, but bring them to a school and they'll feel right at home. Nothing could be further from the truth. Teaching today is vastly different from even a few decades ago. The rise of technology, changes in instructional approaches, and a greater understanding of how we learn have all transformed the field of education.

Just as there are misconceptions about what we think teaching involves, so is our view of learning adversely affected by its illusory nature. Consider, for instance, the following:

- **Learning is primarily memorisation:** Many people associate learning with the ability to recall isolated facts. Yes, memorisation is a component of learning, and is actually often a prerequisite for further learning and problem solving. Without this memorised knowledge, further higher-order learning is impossible.

- **Memorisation is drill and kill:** People associate memorisation with 'drill and kill', a teaching technique where students are repeatedly drilled on the same material, killing their motivation. Critics here also argue that memorisation emphasises factual learning at the expense of deeper understanding and application, whereby students can recall information for a test but don't truly comprehend the material or know how to apply it in different contexts. The fact is that most children love repetition (think of reading nursery rhymes or stories) as it gives them a feeling of accomplishment. By the way, this memorisation creates room in our working memory to allow for deep processing.

- **Faster learning is better:** Many people feel that learning should be made as easy and quick as possible. However, deep, meaningful learning often requires a lot of mental effort as well as time for reflection and integration of new knowledge.
- **Education ends after graduation:** Learning is often viewed as something that happens within the walls of a classroom. In reality, learning is a lifelong process that occurs in various contexts and doesn't stop when formal education ends.
- **Academic performance is the sole indicator of learning:** Grades and test results are often seen as the primary measure of a student's learning, but they don't always reflect a student's understanding, creativity, or practical skills. There's quite a difference between learning and performing.
- **If children learn to speak without explicit instruction, use this approach for learning to read:** Many pedagogues look at how young children learn to orally communicate with each other and then transfer this to learning to read and write. In reality, communication is biologically/evolutionarily primary. It is hard-wired in our evolution and, thus, doesn't require explicit instruction, while reading and writing are cultural artefacts that are biologically/evolutionarily secondary and require explicit instruction.

As you can see, education is both primed for and rife with illusory factors that lead us to misinterpret, oversimplify, or distort. Nevertheless, we want to clear up two important distinctions before we get started:

1. The subject of this book is illusions, not illusionists. In other words, we don't consider teachers or teaching itself to be engaged in any deliberate act of deception. Rather, the nature of teaching and learning itself is susceptible to illusory misinterpretation, and that will be the subject of our scrutiny.
2. The ideas we will explore are illusions, not myths. Though much has been written about the scourge of edu-myths like learning styles or learning pyramids, the ideas we explore are not merely characterised as debunked. They are instead cases in which the outward appearance of effectiveness masks a deeper truth about what really works and why.

As such, our task is not to slay myths but to lift the veil on aspects of education that appear to make sense but, upon closer inspection, prove to be much more complex than meets the eye. For when we bring an evidentiary lens to bear on instructional illusions, we reveal secrets that have been hiding in plain sight all along.

1. The engagement illusion

> 'The universe is full of magical things patiently waiting for our wits to grow sharper.'[5]

In Lewis Carroll's *Through the Looking-Glass, And What Alice Found There*, Alice finds herself in a most peculiar race alongside the Red Queen; a race embodying a profound paradoxical illusion. Despite her breathless exertion and relentless forward motion, Alice remains fixed in space. When Alice expresses bewilderment at this contradiction, the Queen responds: 'It takes all the running you can do, to keep in the same place. If you want to get somewhere else, you must run at least twice as fast as that!' The Red Queen's race represents the peculiar condition where constant motion belies actual progress; where kinetic energy dissipates without producing any meaningful advancement.

Perhaps nowhere is this metaphorical framework more illuminating than in contemporary educational practice in which the classroom, with its carousel of activities, constant hum of discussion, and often-performative busyness, presents us with an illusion so compelling that even the keenest of observers can be tripped up by its dissembling nature. Students transition between stations, manipulate materials, engage in animated dialogue, and produce tangible artefacts of their efforts. However, like Alice, many are cognitively immobile.

When encountering lessons of this nature, one could be forgiven for thinking that a transformative process must be visible in its unfolding. We instinctively associate action with performance; movement with mastery. Our pedagogical intuitions, shaped by cultural conditioning, lead us to conflate the *appearance* of learning with its actual occurrence. Like the audience at a skilled illusionist's performance, we are neurologically predisposed to interpret what we see on the surface as the same as what's happening underneath, even as the real mechanisms remain obscured from view.

The illusion

The engagement illusion is therefore a form of educational *pareidolia*, since it relies on the tendency for us to perceive meaningful patterns where none exist. This cognitive bias is particularly pernicious because it creates a self-reinforcing feedback loop: activities that generate visible engagement receive positive reinforcement from students, colleagues, and parents alike, regardless of their efficacy in producing durable learning.

On one hand, student engagement seems like an obvious prerequisite for learning. After all, how can students learn if they aren't engaged with the material? Educational theorists have long emphasised the importance of student involvement, and teachers worldwide recognise the value of capturing their students' attention and interest. When observers enter classrooms, they often look for signs of engagement as proxies for effective teaching and learning.

On the other hand, research reveals that the appearance of engagement often has little correlation with actual learning. Students can appear thoroughly engaged while learning nothing new, or seem disengaged while profound learning is occurring. The activities that produce the most visible engagement – colourful sorting tasks, animated discussions, interactive games – frequently yield the least durable learning outcomes. Meanwhile, the cognitive processes that lead to deep, lasting learning – struggle, deliberate practice, focused attention on challenging material – may not manifest as obvious 'engagement' at all.

In other words, what looks like learning and what actually promotes learning are frequently at odds with one another.

> 'Students can be busiest and most involved with material they already know.'[6] *Graham Nuthall.*

Nuthall's research underscores how students often engage in tasks that create the illusion of learning but may ultimately be superficial and fail to promote long-term retention. Moreover, a student's prior knowledge within a given domain is the most significant factor in shaping their learning trajectory. As Tricot and Sweller emphasise, 'When performing a cognitive task requiring domain-specific knowledge, the presence or absence of this knowledge is the best predictor of performance.'[7] Without a clear understanding of what students already know or do not know, teachers risk providing activities that do not meaningfully deepen understanding – what appears to be learning may simply be busywork.

Nicholas Soderstrom and Robert Bjork further distinguish between learning and performance. While performance reflects short-term outcomes (such as test scores), learning is about long-term retention and the ability to apply knowledge in the future.[8] The idea that learning is something visibly observable in the classroom is misleading, and as Rob Coe points out, engagement is often a poor indicator of actual learning. Teachers may fall into the trap of assuming that 'I have taught it' is equivalent to 'they have learnt it' without any objective measure of what, if anything, has truly been retained.[9]

This is where the science of learning becomes invaluable – it helps us move beyond cognitive biases and focus on what truly matters. As Soderstrom and Bjork caution, 'How we learn is often vastly misaligned with our metacognitive assessments of how we think we learn.' Understanding these distinctions enables educators to design instruction that fosters genuine, long-lasting learning rather than just temporary performance gains.

The illusion manifests in various ways:

1. **Activity without progress:** Students completing numerous worksheets, making colourful posters, or participating in animated discussions without necessarily developing deeper understanding of core concepts.
2. **Emotional versus cognitive engagement:** Students enjoying an activity (emotional engagement) doesn't guarantee they're processing information in ways that lead to durable learning (cognitive engagement).
3. **The familiarity trap:** Students gravitating toward and appearing most engaged with content they already understand, rather than stretching into challenging new territory.
4. **The performance illusion:** As Soderstrom and Bjork have demonstrated, short-term performance (what students can do during class) is a poor predictor of long-term learning (what they'll remember weeks or months later).

Teachers are particularly susceptible to this fallacy because the feedback is immediate and positive. A classroom of visibly engaged students provides instant gratification and validation. Parents appreciate hearing that their children are engaged in class. Administrators entering for observations are reassured by the sight of students actively participating. Yet this feedback loop can reinforce instructional choices that prioritise visible engagement over lasting learning.

Unmasking the illusion

Unmasking this illusion requires reconceptualising engagement not as an observable state but as an internal cognitive process. In order to grasp what this means, let's first turn our attention to the structure of memory itself.

We know for instance that our working memory (the site of thinking) is notoriously finite and that we can only hold around 4–7 items in it at any moment. By comparison, our long-term memory (the storage facility for encoded knowledge items) is, as far as we know, infinite. One way of thinking about this is to consider your long-term memory as a giant aircraft hangar, and your working memory as a single, tiny letterbox on the front door of the hangar. As we encounter information (in this analogy, the letters being posted through the box), it really matters how we think about that content, especially if ideas are to make their way through the letterbox of our limited working memory and into the hangar of long-term memory.

For this process to result in deep durable learning, it's not enough for students to think about ideas in a superficial manner. Instead, students should be invited to analyse, justify, and provide detailed explanations for core content. Otherwise it's unlikely that they will encode it for future use.

This nature of thought is often referred to by cognitive scientists as *effortful thinking*, and it has at least three important characteristics:

1. **It's difficult, but in a good way:** This looks like students engaging in cognitively demanding tasks about key content, in service of deepened understanding. They do this by asking themselves, 'What lies *beneath the surface* of this idea?'
2. **It calls on the learner to attribute meaning**: This looks like students going beyond the passive, arbitrary encountering of information. They do this by asking themselves, 'What is *significant* about this idea; why does it *matter*?'

3. **It's connected to other parts of learning:** This looks like students considering an idea not as a singularity but as possessing many facets that can be plugged into a larger network of interconnected ideas. They do this by asking themselves, 'What about this idea *can be connected or related to things I already know*?'

Knowing that true engagement happens in the mind and not necessarily in visible behaviour has significant implications for how teachers teach.

Here are several approaches we might use to navigate this challenge:

1. **Distinguish between types of engagement:** Recognise the difference between behavioural engagement (being on task), emotional engagement (enjoying the activity), and cognitive engagement (mentally processing information in ways that lead to learning). Only the last reliably predicts learning outcomes.
2. **Focus on desirable difficulties:** Embrace instructional approaches that make learning appropriately challenging. As Elizabeth and Robert Bjork have demonstrated, strategies that create 'desirable difficulties' – like spaced practice, interleaving, and generation – enhance long-term learning even though they may appear to reduce engagement and performance in the moment.
3. **Design tasks that target what matters:** Create learning activities that direct students' attention to the underlying principles and concepts rather than surface features. For example, rather than having students sort examples into categories, have them compare examples and non-examples to identify distinguishing features.
4. **Use formative assessment:** Rather than relying on visible engagement as evidence of learning, use frequent low-stakes assessments to gauge what students actually know and can do. This provides more reliable feedback than observations of engagement.
5. **Delay judgement of success:** Resist the temptation to judge a lesson's success by immediate student feedback or visible engagement. Instead, assess learning after a delay, when temporary performance effects have worn off and only durable learning remains.
6. **Explain the process to students:** Help students understand that learning doesn't always feel good in the moment. Activities that lead to lasting learning often feel challenging and may not be as immediately rewarding as easier tasks.

To show you what we mean, consider two mathematics lessons on algebraic equations.

In the first, students rotate through colourful stations with manipulatives, creating visual models of equations, playing equation-matching games, and working collaboratively to solve puzzles. The room buzzes with activity and discussion.

In the second, students work quietly through a carefully sequenced set of increasingly difficult equations with periodic teacher guidance, frequent checking for understanding, and deliberate practice of key skills. The room is relatively quiet, punctuated by moments of teacher explanation and questioning.

The first classroom appears more 'engaged' to an observer, but research suggests the second approach is more likely to yield durable learning. The engagement fallacy leads us to favour the first approach despite evidence favouring the second.

Conclusion

Ultimately, overcoming the engagement illusion requires a shift in mindset, from valuing what looks like learning to prioritising what actually leads to long-term understanding. While student participation and enthusiasm are important, they are not reliable indicators of deep learning. Effective teaching is not about creating the most visually stimulating classroom, but about designing instruction that challenges students to think deeply, make connections, and engage in effortful cognitive work.

2. The expertise illusion

'There are known knowns. These are things we know that we know. There are known unknowns. That is to say, there are things that we know we don't know. But there are also unknown unknowns. There are things we don't know we don't know.'[10]

Have you ever been so sure of something that you couldn't imagine anyone holding the opposing view? The sky is blue, the sun is hot, and no one will ever emulate the feats of Sir Alex Ferguson during his wildly successful 26-year reign as manager of Manchester United. All realities that we can reliably hold as givens in an otherwise uncertain world. But what if it turned out you couldn't be so sure? What if something new came along and shook the foundations of your supposedly clear and objective view of reality?

Becoming an expert involves being open to such revelations and the humility that comes with them. As the saying goes: when we know better, we can do better. The problem is, we don't always know whether what we know is all there is to know, ya know? This tendency is common among conspiracy theorists, whose misguided views are immovable even in the face of overwhelming evidence to the contrary. In one example from social media (which I hasten to add is likely a parody) a post read, 'The Flat Earth Society has members all around the globe,' reminding us that the call for irrefutable evidence is sometimes coming from inside the house.

Interestingly, research tells us that an abundance of expertise also has its drawbacks. That is to say, knowledge can often act like a curse that leaves experts blind to the perspectives of those less in the know. Notions of expertise and novicehood therefore appear straightforward on the surface, but once we explore each through the lens of research, we begin to reveal the counterintuitive features that hide behind the illusion.

The illusion

At the heart of this illusion is the idea that expertise is a double-edged sword. On the one hand, being a novice means we mischaracterise our abilities, while being an expert diminishes our ability to communicate our expertise to others. We might refer to these phenomena as the curse of knowing too little and the curse of knowing too much.

The curse of knowing too little

The limitations of limited knowledge have long been the subject of study within the field of educational psychology. Starting with Kurt Lewin in the early 1900s and latterly Jean Piaget, researchers were concerned with the idea that humans are trapped in a kind of egocentric echo chamber that makes it difficult for them to see the totality of what there is to know. We conflate subjective and objective interpretations of the world around us, assuming that *our* version is closer to *the* version than is actually the case. Over time, these theories put forward by Lewin and Piaget crystallised into what we now know as *naïve realism*.[11]

According to the naïve realists, our problems begin the moment we assume that what we see is objective truth, since this assurance in our objectivity throws any attempt at perspective-taking into chaos. As with our opening example, one can imagine how this plays out on social media, where even the most outlandish theories are afforded the lustre of legitimacy. After all, whenever I post online that the world is flat, I receive countless reinforcing affirmations that I must be right.

In addition to the conflation principle found in naïve realism, we also tend to inflate our perceived expertise, a phenomenon referred to as the *Dunning–Kruger effect*. David Dunning and Justin Kruger's seminal study 'Unskilled and unaware of it'[12] found that individuals who perform in the bottom quartile of a particular domain tend to significantly overestimate their abilities, even claiming that they are above average. For Dunning and Kruger, 'Not only do these people reach erroneous conclusions and make unfortunate choices, but their incompetence robs them of the metacognitive ability to realize it.' What's more, their studies found that when participants improved their skills and knowledge in a given domain, they became more accurate in determining their abilities in that regard.

More recent research has added to the ill effects of Dunning–Kruger-style over-inflation, suggesting that a lack of knowledge also invites us to believe that we have all the information we'll need, a phenomenon known as *the illusion of information adequacy*.[13] In one study, researchers presented participants with a dilemma: whether a school with limited access to water should stay put and hope for rain or merge with another school that has an abundance of water. In the study, one group of participants was given a full account of all the information necessary to make the decision (including both pro-merge and pro-separation arguments) while two other groups were only given information that supported one side of the debate. In each case, the pro-merge and pro-separation groups felt as though they had enough knowledge to make an informed decision, even though they weren't provided with sufficient information to do so. However, even when participants were provided with the full suite of pro-merge *and* pro-separation arguments (knowledge that the control group had been privy to all along) a majority of those participants stuck with their original decision – the one based on incomplete information. So, it seems we have three problems that can play out whenever we lack knowledge:

1. We confuse our subjective knowledge with objective reality.
2. We overestimate what we think we know.
3. We assume we have all the information we need.

Before we explore what to do about that, let's explore the other side of the problem.

The curse of knowing too much

One might assume, given the scourge of knowing too little, that knowing too much would only be a good thing. Unfortunately, when we look at the evidence, that does not always appear to be the case.

Indeed, what we have come to know as *the curse of knowledge* has its roots in the way experts and novices fundamentally differ. Contrary to how we might intuitively understand it, experts don't simply know more than novices. Knowledge is not rendered as a simple list of facts. Rather, experts organise knowledge differently than novices, creating interconnected webs of knowledge items referred to as schemas. We all possess schemas of one type or another but an expert schema is more sophisticated, meaning experts can do more with what they have. For instance, experts can look beyond the surface phenomena of an idea and see its underlying architecture, meaning they can establish points of connection between ideas that may appear different to the uninitiated observer. In other words, experts can organise, synthesise, and otherwise manipulate information in ways that novices cannot.

Imagine, then, what happens when an expert attempts to teach a novice. Well, it turns out the effects can be just as damaging as the curse of knowing too little. Researchers have shown how humans tend to use heuristics (or mental shortcuts) to support them in predicting how much others know about a given subject.[14] Like any cognitive shortcut, the cost of assuming how much someone knows can lead to a more efficient but ultimately misguided approximation of their abilities.

In one recent study, researchers presented participants with a series of trivia questions and asked them to estimate the extent to which novices in those subject areas would know the answers.[15] Researchers then gave participants the opportunity to study subjects on the test and discovered something interesting: the more participants came to know about the trivia topics, the less effective they became at predicting how relative novices would fare on those questions.

Just as with knowing too little, knowing too much possesses its own flaws:

1. Experts don't just know more than novices; they see things differently and organise information in an entirely different way.
2. Experts tend to make faulty assumptions about what novices do and don't know.
3. The more expert we become, the harder it is to appreciate a novice's level of understanding.

What are we to do about this damned-if-you-know, damned-if-you-don't dilemma established by decades of research into the role of expertise in learning? How can we navigate this seeming contradiction while still acknowledging the strengths and flaws of the expert and novice alike?

Unmasking the illusion

When it comes to ameliorating these effects, much can be won and lost before the teacher has even entered the classroom. Here we will explore two strategies a teacher can employ when planning to teach: lesson internalisation and the use of examples and non-examples in instructional design.

Bridging the gap between experts and novices through lesson internalisation

When planning a lesson or unit of study, it's important to internalise that which you are about to teach. Lesson internalisation essentially means walking through the lesson from a student's point of view in order to predict how the content will be experienced. In turn, lesson internalisation allows the teacher to make accommodations and seize upon opportunities for learning – a process that is even more critical when one considers the expert–novice divide that exists between teachers and students.

The steps teachers take to internalise don't come about by happenstance (they require intentionality of process), and they can easily be misconstrued or brushed over (they require a fidelity of implementation). In other words, if you think skimming through a lesson plan to get the gist of what you want students to learn will suffice, you should probably think again.

Instead, consider using lesson internalisation to address the expert–novice divide by asking the following questions:

- **What do the students actually know?** This step involves becoming aware that students come with different levels of background knowledge and then determining what that knowledge is.

- **What am I asking students to do?** This step means completing the activities you're expecting your students to engage in, a process known as *cognitive task analysis*.[16] After all, if you don't know exactly what they will be expected to do, how will you know whether they have what they need to do it?

- **What will students need to know and be able to do in order to engage in the task?** This is where the first seducing influences of the curse of knowledge can come in. To avoid misappropriating student expertise, you'll need to break down the items of knowledge into careful causal structures (e.g., in order for my students to be able to do C, they will have to understand and be able to use precursory knowledge items A and B).

- **What is this learning building towards?** As a counterpoint to the previous step, this calls on you to fit the here-and-now of the lesson into the broader arc of learning (e.g., I'm covering A, B, and C in this way because I know the students will need it for D and E). In other words, if you don't know where the learning is going, you can't put in place the foundations necessary for supporting that future learning.

- **How might students struggle?** This step requires you to appreciate how students might get things wrong rather than assuming that they know it all in the same way that you do. This means determining student misconceptions by saying to yourself, 'I know for a fact that students have tended to confuse X with Y, so I need to be alive to that and have a clarifying explanation ready to go.'

- **How might students succeed?** This step allows you to look for all the opportunities students will have to make gains in the topic. For instance, you can identify the 1–3 key knowledge items you want students to be able to take away and, in concert with the steps outlined above, determine which supports, scaffolds, and searching questions you may want to employ to drive those key ideas home.

Bridging the gap between experts and novices through examples and non-examples

Examples and non-examples are a great tool since they invite us to break down ideas into their constituent parts and to show what something is by virtue of what it isn't. Arriving at this level of precision is important because of another challenge faced by experts: *conversational implicature*.

Conversational implicature could be colloquially referred to any imprecise language used by someone attempting to explain a new idea. In the hands of an expert such abstractness isn't necessarily costly (since they already have the gist) but for novices such lack of clarity can be catastrophic. For instance, imagine someone was learning to fly a plane and their instructor asked them to 'angle the nose of the plane a touch downwards'. For the expert, the language of 'a touch' has a degree of significance that comes with the territory. They know what 'a touch' means within the context of keeping the plan stable. For the novice, such an instruction could mean anything from a minor adjustment to an irretrievable nosedive, and unless the expert can explain *exactly* what they mean, it leaves it open to chance that the novice will fall foul of the ambiguity.

To ameliorate the ill effects of conversational implicature, examples and non-examples work by keeping bright the boundaries between concepts and gradations of meaning. One example (shared by Jim's wonderful colleague and co-author Rebekah Berlin) deals with teaching a youngster how to use a hammer. In such a case, it wouldn't be enough to simply say, 'Start by holding the hammer so that it feels comfortable in your hand,' and expect the novice to know what 'comfortable' means in this case. Instead we might consider saying, 'Try holding the hammer high up on the handle and notice how it doesn't give you much power. Now try holding the hammer lower down on the handle and notice how it doesn't give you much control. Now practise finding a place between those extremes that gives you a happy balance of power *and* control.' Notice here how the ambiguity of 'comfortable' gives way to the sweet-spot precision afforded by the non-examples on either side.

Examples and non-examples also invite experts to reconsider and understand afresh what makes a knowledge item work in the first place. For example, consider the following three images and ask yourself: which of these is a square?

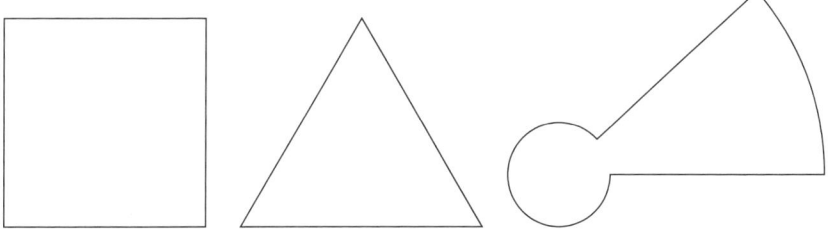

It might be clear to everyone above the age of two that the first shape is an example of a square and the second image is a non-example of a square, but what of the final one?

It turns out that the third image could in fact be a square. After all, it has four sides of equal length and four right angles. In this case, even if you were a relative 'expert' in knowing what makes a square a square, the act of working through the example, the non-example, and the unlikely example invites us to reconsider what a square even is to begin with. It's this brand of back-to-fundamentals thinking that experts need to be able to do if they hope to meet novices where they are.

Conclusion

We started this chapter by stating that experts and novices are each trapped in a kind of cognitive constraint that impedes the effective transfer of knowledge. Experts, it seems, can't help but be experts – a reality that renders them unable to see the world through a novice's eyes.

Novices, for their part, are hoodwinked by their own lack of knowledge and understanding – leading to critical flaws in how they make meaning and subsequently learn.

Like many acts of intellectual rigour, the key to undoing this bind is to not take knowledge for granted. This requires us to be intentional in making the familiar unfamiliar, to encounter new ideas with the wide-eyed, open-mindedness of the uninitiated, and to teach in such a way that acknowledges the expert–novice divide can indeed be bridged.

3. The student-centred illusion

> *'We choose to give people autonomy within a frame, with full understanding that some people are going to struggle to use that autonomy well.'*[17]

In his autobiography, *My Life and Work*, Henry Ford recalls a sales meeting from 1909 when the question of which colours to paint the Model T Ford was brought to the table. As a pioneer of mass production, Ford recognised the inefficiencies that would result from offering the Model T in a range of hues. He knew that black was the cheapest paint available, and that casting his cars in additional colours would require the assembly line to be halted and reconfigured for each new shade. In response to a claim from his team that this would offer consumers limited choice and adversely impact sales, Ford famously replied, 'Any customer can have a car painted any color that [he] wants, so long as it is black.'[18]

Ford's quip is an example of what some refer to as *bounded autonomy*. This is the idea that certain conditions provide people with a degree of freedom (the freedom to buy a car and to have it in any colour you like) while situating that freedom within a set of predetermined boundaries (as long as the colour of the car is black). Notions of bounded autonomy also play out in educational settings, especially when student freedom to 'own' their learning is set in opposition with the teacher's responsibility for that learning – and few tensions are more prominent in education than that of teacher-led instruction versus student-centred learning.

The illusion

The debate between teacher-led instruction and student-centred learning has long raged in education circles. In the red corner we have the 'sage on the stage', whose primary role is to impart knowledge while students sit silently in rows and passively take note of the wisdom being imparted. In the blue corner, we have the 'guide on the side', there to create the conditions in which students learn from one another. In this case, students are put in groups, normally with allocated roles like 'timekeeper' and 'scribe', before undertaking a choose-your-own-adventure task in which they supposedly guide one another towards new knowledge.

This divide doesn't only play out at a pedagogical level. It can also communicate a philosophical and (dare we say) political disposition in the eye of the beholder. For some, advocating for teacher-led approaches is tantamount to a 'trad' take on education, seemingly drawing on a brand of conservatism that calls for children to be seen and not heard. Meanwhile, the student-centred advocates are pigeonholed as 'progs' whose politics are more akin to free-range childhood development and the empowering of students as teachers unto themselves – and herein lies the heart of the illusion. In reality, any deep exploration of how learning happens reveals the teacher-led versus student-centred debate to be a false binary that caricatures both sides and leaves little room for nuance.

Indeed, educational researchers and theorists have wrestled with the tension between teacher-led and student-centred approaches, including Jere Brophy and Thomas L. Good in their seminal work 'Teacher behavior and student achievement'.[19] At a fundamental level, Brophy and Good define effective teachers as 'Conveyors of Information … determined by how they structure and sequence ideas.' What's more, they explain how 'students achieve more in classes where they spend most of their time being taught or supervised by their teachers rather than working on their own'. If this was the entirety of their case, it would be reasonable to conclude: so far, so teacher-led. However, Brophy and Good also go on to say that 'the teacher carries the content to the students personally … but conveys information mostly in brief presentations followed by recitation or application opportunities'. This conclusion establishes a different take, in which students are ultimately expected to do something with what they are coming to know, hence placing them more centrally responsible for their own learning.

So, where does this leave us? If even the experts appear conflicted in the face of the teacher-led, student-centred illusion, what are we to do? To answer this question, let's return to what cognitive scientists refer to as *schema theory*.

Schemas and the acquisition of new knowledge

As already explored, we know that learners don't acquire and organise knowledge as a series of isolated facts like a shopping list. In fact, knowledge is organised in networks of interconnected ideas, more like a family tree. These networks are known as schemas, and the more we come to know about a particular domain of knowledge, the more sophisticated that schema becomes.

We see schemas at work whenever people encounter new information, since all new information needs somewhere to land and live within our existing understanding of the world. For instance, imagine you showed a 2-year-old child a picture of an airplane and they mischaracterised it as a helicopter. The root of their mischaracterisation would exist somewhere in their (as yet) faulty schematic understanding of the concept. The child would have made connections to what they already know (it's a man-made flying object that carries passengers in the sky) but would nevertheless have missed its exact categorisation as a helicopter.

Now imagine that this same 2-year-old grew up to become an aeronautical engineer. Not only would they know the difference between an airplane and a helicopter, but they would also appreciate all the nuanced distinctions between the two, including their means of propulsion, engine types, turning capabilities, and fuel consumption. In other words, they would know all the things that make a helicopter a helicopter, and all the things that make an airplane an airplane.

This is significant because it underscores two important truths about learning:

1. Learners come to understand new information by reference to what they already know.
2. Learners will activate their prior knowledge either way, even if that knowledge happens to be incomplete or inaccurate.[20]

All of which invites a question that can help us to address the teacher-led, student-centred dilemma: how can teachers meet learners where they are *and* ensure they activate prior knowledge that will best support them in new learning?

Activating the right kind of prior knowledge

To understand how prior knowledge activation works, we must first explore what happens when it doesn't work. After all, if students are going to activate all manner of potentially distracting prior knowledge, it follows that a number of potential pitfalls would need to be avoided.

For instance, imagine you're teaching an English class to a group of 10- and 11-year-olds on the subject of pathetic fallacy. You want students to know that pathetic fallacy is when a writer imbues inanimate objects with human emotions to reflect the mood of a character or story (e.g., the sun was smiling down on us). You also want students to recognise pathetic fallacy within a text, justify how the device contributes to textual meaning, and ultimately craft their own pathetic fallacy constructions.

Before students can take on the above learning goals, however, they need to understand the concept at the core – namely, a working definition of pathetic fallacy. In order to do so, students will need to activate prior knowledge along the way, which is where pitfalls can come in.

One pitfall can best be described as **'missing by a mile'**. This is when a learner activates prior knowledge that has nothing to do with the target content at hand. In the case of our English lesson, this could involve a student saying something like 'Oh cool! My favourite heavy metal band is called Pathetic Fallacy. This lesson is going to be great! Rock on!' With this as the student's foundation, any attempt to explain and explore the target content for the lesson will have to push directly against this rogue prior knowledge. Like trying to force a puzzle piece where it doesn't belong, the student is likely to toil with futility at the chalkface of the idea, unless the teacher sets their misconception straight.

A second pitfall for prior knowledge activation might be referred to as **'knowing just enough to be dangerous'**. This is when the student has a marginal understanding of the material and enough prior knowledge to make a partial connection, but the connection is too tangential or underdeveloped to be useful. In our pathetic fallacy example, this would involve a student saying something like 'Oh I know what this is: the word pathetic means "weak" or "sad" so this must be to do with depicting a character or situation as feeble in nature'. Even though this is an earnest attempt at connecting new information to prior knowledge, there's a fundamental disconnect that is akin to the airplane/helicopter example provided earlier. If left alone, this student would likely connect and encode the irrelevant information. Just like a bug in a computer, this information will then go on to corrupt future learning, since the student would build new parts of knowledge on top of this faulty foundation.

A third prior-knowledge pitfall could best be referred to as the '**hiding in plain sight**' problem. This is when a student possesses accurate, relevant prior knowledge but it remains inactivated. In our example, this might look like the student saying, 'I know that the Greek word "pathos" can mean "emotion" or "experience". Is that significant?' An effective teacher would be ready to pounce on this moment of connection. The student's observation that pathos forms part of the word pathetic, which lends meaning to our emerging understanding of pathetic fallacy, is precisely the prior knowledge that will assist their learning. Yet, if this meaningful connection is missed, then the diamond will remain in the rough and the opportunity to learn will pass.

Unmasking the illusion

If we as teachers are to meet students where they are and support their learning, it requires us to acknowledge their prior knowledge (i.e., to centre learning around what the students already know) and invite them to connect new information to their prior knowledge (i.e., to teach in ways that take full advantage of what students already know). In other words, when teachers take prior knowledge and schemas into account, it helps place students at the centre of learning *and* requires an intentional, teacher-led process.

So, what does this look like in practice? How can we walk the practice of teacher-led instruction and chew the gum of student-centred learning at the same time? What pedagogical practices would allow us to refute the illusion at the centre of this chapter?

One powerful strategy can be summed up in three words: *make schemas explicit*. This is to say, instead of shrouding helpful prior knowledge, make those connections visible and encourage students to do the same. To show what that might look like, imagine you're teaching a lesson on the causes of World War I in preparation for a forthcoming essay on the topic. You have already covered the main causes but you ultimately want students to synthesise those reasons into meaningful categories rather than see them as isolated facts.

You *could* ask students to work with a partner and set a challenge to list as many causes as possible, with a prize for the winning team. Such an approach would violate our understanding of how information is integrated and organised in relation to what we already know. By having students make a list, there is no invitation to see the causes of World War I as interconnected. As a result, any chance students had to make explicit schematic relationships would be lost, as would the opportunity to reveal and capitalise on any meaningful prior knowledge students might have at their disposal.

Now let's imagine a different approach. Instead of having students make a list of the causes of World War I, you provide them with a set of cards, each of which states a cause for the war. The first job is for each student to organise the cards into categories of their choosing, as well as write out any additional cards not represented in the deck. You then ask students to work with a partner or small group to justify their choices, at which point the class would come together to establish a final set of contributing categories. In so doing, the teacher makes explicit the parts of knowledge that need to be synthesised so that students can make explicit their own schema via the categorisation task. This helps students encode the information they are coming to know into a well-organised schema, and helps the teacher to spot any potential prior knowledge flaws or pitfalls that might corrupt their emergent understanding of the topic.

Conclusion

As we consider this example, our understanding of schemas, and the importance of prior knowledge activation in general, a few things become clear:

- Students should be at the centre of learning – as the primary beneficiaries of it – but this doesn't mean students should be primarily responsible for all the learning that needs to happen.
- At the same time, just because a teacher thinks they taught it doesn't mean a student has learned it.
- Rather than using the above to drive an unnecessary wedge between teacher-led instruction and student-centred learning, we can achieve both whenever:
  - teachers appreciate how students come to understand new information by reference to what they already know.
  - teachers activate students' prior knowledge in ways that build towards an understanding of new material.
  - teachers invite students to make visible the schematic organisation of concepts when activating prior knowledge.

These considerations are critical for equitable instruction. After all, if prior knowledge activation is a case of 'it takes one to know one' then we need to ensure that all students have the opportunity to connect accurate, relevant prior knowledge to new learning. If we do so, then it can safely be said that effective teacher-led instruction is student-centred.

4. The transfer illusion

'Practice in context, perform in context.'[21]

Consider a student learning to bake a sourdough loaf in a cookery class. They learn each discrete step: feeding the starter, mixing the dough, the precise temperatures, the folding techniques, the proofing times. In the controlled environment of a cooking class, with premeasured ingredients and perfect conditions, they produce an admirable loaf. The recipe becomes a seemingly straightforward formula: combine A with B, wait X minutes, perform Y folds, maintain Z temperature.

Yet when this same student attempts to bake at home, something shifts. Their kitchen is cooler than the classroom, affecting fermentation times. Their starter behaves differently in winter than summer. The flour from their local store has a different protein content than the one used in class, and suddenly the precise formula that worked so well in controlled conditions fails to produce the same results in a new context. The bread is dense, underproofed, the crust either pale or burnt. Although the student was able to bake a loaf in the short term and was confident how to do it again, this did not lead to them being able to bake bread at home even though they felt they had used the same steps; what was 'learned' in one context did not transfer to another.

This illusion illustrates a fundamental challenge in learning and instructional design: the gap between controlled learning and real-world application often referred to as 'transfer'. Transfer of learning refers to the ability to apply knowledge, skills, or principles learned in one context to a different, novel situation. It is a fundamental goal of education, ensuring that learning extends beyond its original setting to real-world applications. Transfer can be near (applying learning to a highly similar context) or far (applying learning to a vastly different context), and its success depends on recognising underlying principles rather than merely memorising procedures.

Just as our baker must learn to 'read' the dough and adapt to subtle variations and unexpected changes rather than rigidly follow steps, students must develop the ability to transfer knowledge to contexts beyond the original one. Real mastery in applying learning isn't about just memorising and unthinkingly carrying out procedures but understanding underlying principles that remain constant while the variables can change. A skilled baker knows how temperature affects fermentation, how different flours absorb water differently, and how to adjust proofing times based on environmental conditions. They've developed what Donald Schön calls 'reflection-in-action'.[22] In other words, the ability to think on their feet and adjust their approach based on changing circumstances.

The illusion

The transfer illusion represents one of education's deceptive trade-offs: optimising between immediate performance and long-term application. This tension manifests in the recurring challenge educators face – whether to teach for mastery within a specific context or to cultivate broader, more flexible understanding that can bridge multiple domains. It also underlines another counterintuitive fact about learning and instruction; in order to get something, surely you should do more of that thing? However, as we have explored before, problem solving is a bad way for novices to learn how to solve problems.[23]

This illusion is not a modern one, however. Aristotle's categorical reasoning system provided the first systematic framework for addressing this challenge. His approach went far beyond simple classification; it established a sophisticated methodology for understanding how the mind recognises and transfers patterns across contexts. Through his *Categories*,[24] Aristotle identified fundamental types of knowledge – substance, quantity, quality, and relation – that he believed represented universal structures underlying all learning. These categories weren't merely organisational tools but represented what he saw as the basic building blocks of transferable knowledge.

His theory of proportional analogy (A:B :: C:D) offered a concrete mechanism for understanding how knowledge bridges domains. When a student grasps that the relationship between a circle's diameter and circumference mirrors the relationship between a sphere's surface area and volume, they're engaging in exactly the kind of structural pattern recognition that enables transfer. This approach suggested that true understanding involves recognising not just surface similarities but deeper relational patterns – an insight that presaged modern cognitive theories of transfer.

The enduring relevance of Aristotle's framework lies in its recognition that effective transfer requires both analytical tools for breaking down knowledge into constituent elements and then adaptive capabilities for reassembling these elements in new contexts. This dual emphasis on analysis and synthesis continues to influence contemporary approaches to transfer, from Gentner's structure-mapping theory[25] (the idea that analogical reasoning works by mapping deep relational structures between concepts), to modern computational models of analogical reasoning. The tension he identified between specific knowledge and generalisable understanding remains at the heart of the transfer illusion, informing current debates about how to balance contextual learning with abstract principle formation.

In the modern era, the empirical investigation of transfer began with Thorndike's 1901 theory of identical elements, where his crucial insight was the suggestion that the transfer of learning depends on the degree of similarity between the original learning situation and the new application context. According to this theory, transfer is most likely when two tasks share common elements – be they cognitive, procedural, or perceptual.[26] This had profound implications for education and training, as it implied that knowledge and skills learned in one context may not automatically generalise to another, especially if the contexts appear superficially different. Thorndike's early experiments revealed a sobering reality: even when activities appeared logically related, knowledge remained stubbornly bound to its original learning context. This 'contextual imprisonment' of knowledge posed a fundamental challenge to educators – how could they ensure that classroom learning would translate to real-world application?

However, the cognitive revolution of the mid-20th century then brought crucial theoretical advances that began to illuminate possible solutions to the transfer illusion. Roediger's transfer-appropriate processing framework[27] demonstrated why students might excel in classroom tests yet struggle with practical applications: memory performance improves when learning processes match retrieval conditions. This insight suggested that effective transfer required aligning educational experiences more closely with eventual application contexts. Perkins and Salomon[28] further refined our understanding by distinguishing between 'low-road transfer' (automatic, practice-based) and 'high-road transfer' (mindful abstraction), explaining why some skills transfer readily while others demand deliberate bridging strategies.

But learning does not happen in a vacuum. Lave and Wenger's situated learning theory[29] further illuminated the transfer illusion's possible resolution by emphasising knowledge's social and contextual nature. Their research revealed how learning becomes embedded in specific communities of practice, suggesting that transfer strategies must account for both cognitive and social dimensions of knowledge application. In other words, learning is not just an individual cognitive process but a socially situated activity, meaning that knowledge transfer depends as much on the environment, interactions, and cultural context as on the content being learned. This understanding had profound implications for educational design, suggesting that authentic learning environments and apprenticeship models play crucial roles in facilitating transfer.

Yet all these theoretical advances revealed an even deeper paradox: the very conditions that optimise immediate learning may inhibit subsequent transfer. In other words, controlled learning environments like a classroom allow rapid skill acquisition but poorly prepare learners for the messy variability of far transfer and application in the exam hall.

Unmasking the illusion

The transfer illusion reveals a fundamental tension in educational design: the conditions that optimise immediate performance often differ dramatically from those that enable long-term application across diverse contexts. This tension manifests not merely as a continuum of difficulty, but as a complex interplay between contextual factors, cognitive processes, and instructional design elements that collectively determine whether knowledge remains bound to its original learning environment or becomes flexible enough for far transfer.

At the heart of this tension lies the contextual nature of learning itself. Knowledge acquired within highly structured, predictable environments – like the controlled setting of a baking class – often remains 'contextually imprisoned', to borrow Thorndike's phrase. The resolution to this illusion begins with understanding how learning environments can be intentionally designed to cultivate what Hatano and Inagaki termed 'adaptive expertise'[30] – knowledge that retains its utility across changing circumstances.

Recent research has illuminated several pathways through this apparent contradiction. The strategic implementation of contextual variation during initial learning phases proves crucial for developing transferable knowledge structures. Studies examining mathematical problem solving demonstrate that students exposed to diverse contextual applications of the same underlying principles exhibit significantly greater transfer capability than those confined to homogeneous example types. For instance, when learning algebraic equations, students who practise with problems situated across scientific, economic, and geometric contexts demonstrate superior ability to recognise the same underlying structures in novel situations compared to peers who practise within a single domain.

This contextual variation approach aligns with Bjork and Bjork's concept of 'desirable difficulties', where carefully calibrated challenges during learning enhance long-term retention and transfer potential. Interleaving, the practice of mixing different problem types or concepts within a learning session rather than blocking similar problems together, represents a particularly powerful manifestation of this principle. When interleaving mathematical problem types, for example, students must continually shift their attention between different solution strategies, forcing them to develop discrimination skills that identify which principles apply to which contexts. This cognitive challenge initially slows learning but ultimately produces more robust, flexible knowledge structures capable of bridging contextual gaps.

Similarly, the spacing effect, distributing practice across time rather than massing it into single sessions, creates productive retrieval challenges that strengthen the cognitive architecture supporting transfer. By requiring learners to reconstruct knowledge across different temporal contexts, spaced practice builds resilience against the contextual dependencies that often constrain transfer.

The contextual boundaries of knowledge transfer can be further expanded through what van Merriënboer and Kirschner demonstrated in their research on complex learning: presenting problems with calculated variations in surface features while maintaining constant deep structures. This approach develops what might be termed 'boundary-crossing competencies' – metacognitive skills that enable learners to recognise invariant principles across diverse contextual presentations.

In practical terms, this means designing learning experiences where the underlying conceptual structures remain consistent while the contextual elements – the narrative framing, the specific variables, or the application domain – systematically vary. For example, medical students trained through problem-based learning scenarios that maintain consistent pathophysiological principles while varying patient demographics, presenting symptoms, and clinical settings develop superior diagnostic transfer compared to those trained through more traditional, compartmentalised approaches. The variability in context forces learners to abstract the essential elements from their situational trappings – precisely the cognitive skill required for successful transfer.

This careful orchestration of contextual variation represents a middle path between two problematic extremes in educational design: excessive decontextualisation that produces inert knowledge (theoretical understanding without practical application capability), and hyper-contextualisation that creates knowledge so bound to specific situations that it fails to transfer beyond its original context. The resolution lies not in eliminating context, which would strip learning of meaning, but in strategically varying contexts to highlight the invariant principles that persist across situations.

The successful navigation of the transfer illusion thus requires integrating abstract principles with varied concrete applications, bringing together Aristotle's emphasis on conceptual frameworks with Thorndike's identical elements theory. This integration helps learners develop what might be called 'structural perception': the ability to recognise deep patterns beneath surface differences. Just as a mathematician learns to see the same equation expressed in different scenarios, successful transfer requires developing what Gentner described as 'structure-mapping' abilities that map relationships between seemingly disparate domains.

For educators, this suggests a progression in instructional design: beginning with clear exemplars that establish foundational understanding, then systematically introducing contextual variation to develop flexible knowledge structures. This progression might involve what Brown and colleagues termed 'preparation for future learning';[31] developing not just specific knowledge but also the metacognitive capabilities to adapt and extend that knowledge across novel situations.

The transfer illusion thus reveals itself not as a simple trade-off between easy and difficult learning conditions, but as a sophisticated design challenge requiring careful calibration of contextual factors. The resolution lies in creating what might be termed 'transfer-rich' learning environments; settings that simultaneously support immediate performance while developing the cognitive flexibility necessary for knowledge application across diverse contexts. Such environments balance contextual authenticity with principled variation, immediate feedback with productive struggle, and domain-specific knowledge with boundary-crossing competencies.

Conclusion

In returning to our sourdough baker, we see that true mastery emerges not from perfect reproduction of classroom conditions, but from understanding how principles of fermentation, hydration, and gluten development manifest across changing environmental contexts. The expert baker develops what Schön called 'reflection-in-action'; not rigid adherence to formulas but adaptive response to contextual variations, guided by internalised principles that transcend any specific baking environment.

The transfer illusion reminds us that learning design must account for both the immediate context of knowledge acquisition and the diverse contexts of eventual application. Effective transfer requires not just knowledge of what works in one setting, but understanding of why it works and how those principles manifest across different settings, developing not just contextual knowledge but truly transferable understanding.

5. The easy-wins illusion

'All things are difficult before they are easy.'[32]

In 1849, thousands of wide-eyed hopefuls rushed to California dreaming of easy riches, seduced by tales of gold simply waiting to be picked up from streambeds like so many castaway pebbles. This promise of fortune, driven in large part by the press at the time, proved to be far from the truth. The reality involved backbreaking work, with most successful miners spending years developing expertise in complex techniques. This 'easy gold' illusion mirrors a persistent misconception in education, namely that learning can (or ought to be) achievable in a free-and-easy manner.

In reality, anyone who has ever aspired to achieve anything of substance knows that 'it don't come easy'.[33] It's not only a question of practice, practice, practice, but also of pushing the boundaries of what you can do – and pushing those boundaries most often comes with pain and frustration. If you have a good trainer or music teacher, they will make sure that – whether you like it or not – it's no easy journey. A speed skater in the Netherlands practises intervals until they either feel like puking or actually do, and often finds themselves fastened to giant rubber bands and being pulled sideways on a runner's track until they can no longer stand. All of these are part of a training programme set up by their coach and intended to push them to the edge of their capacity. The same is true for anyone who really wants to learn to play an instrument or sing or do anything that calls on us to improve over time. Effective trainers, coaches, and teachers have known this reality all along. It's less a case of 'there's gold in them there hills' and more a matter of 'no pain, no gain'.

The illusion

One of education's most seductive misconceptions is the belief that learning should be effortless. As good people, we try to lighten our neighbour's load. As parents, we want to make things easier for our children than they were for us, though this often goes to extremes: helicopter parents hovering over kids fearing that they experience problems; snowplough parents who seek to remove all obstacles from their child's path so they don't experience pain, failure, or discomfort; and curling parents who sweep away all obstacles in their kid's path so that they can go through life without the slightest bump. As teachers, we sometimes compound this bubble-wrap effect by striving to make learning as easy as possible.

This illusion is particularly persuasive because it aligns with what students think they want: an easy path to success. It manifests in teaching practices that prioritise immediate comprehension over deep understanding, in student evaluation systems that reward quick performance over lasting learning, and in educational technology that promises 'painless' learning over the real work of improving. The immediate results – happy students, good test scores, positive course evaluations – seem to validate this approach but hide a sinister truth.

The reality is that true learning only happens when we expend mental effort during learning. Learning requires deep processing of what we are to learn. And this deep processing requires mental effort. Maybe you've heard of the homo economicus (Latin for 'economic man') who makes decisions on what to do based upon questions like: what's in it for me? Do the costs of doing something weigh up against the benefits I receive if I do it? If the balance shifts to profits, we do it. If it shifts to costs, we don't. A spin-off of this is what can be called the *discipulus economicus*,[34] or as they can be pejoratively called: the calculating student. This is a student who carries out the minimum of effort for the maximum benefit, by asking, 'How can I complete this task with the least amount of mental effort?' The job of the good teacher, thus, is to coax, force, and stimulate their students to expend the necessary mental effort while learning.

There is just one caveat here. Not all extra mental effort leads to increased and deeper learning. Making a task too hard to solve because the learner lacks the prerequisite knowledge to solve it, designing learning to achieve failure, and choosing an instructional approach like discovery learning or inquiry learning all require the learner to expend quite a lot of mental effort, but not necessarily in service of the learning goals or in ways that lead to better learning.

So where are we to go with this illusion? How can we square the circle that learning cannot be so easy or so taxing as to make the learning process futile? Thankfully, cognitive science provides a way to solve this illusory dilemma: desirable difficulties.

Desirable difficulties

Desirable difficulties are learning conditions that are often experienced by the learner as requiring more effort, but that have a positive effect on learning and the transfer of knowledge and skills. In the words of Robert and Elizabeth Bjork, 'Conditions of learning that make performance improve rapidly often fail to support long-term retention and transfer, whereas conditions that create challenges and slow the rate of apparent learning often optimize long-term retention and transfer.'[35] This critical distinction between performance and learning lies at the root of the idea of desirable difficulties. At its most fundamental, learning is a change in our long-term memory.[36] Learning is also lasting and stable, and when 'forgotten', it's still somewhere in your long-term memory so that relearning is possible. Performance (or achievement), on the other hand, is short-term. It's fragile and often quickly forgotten (like right after an inspiring event, test, or exam) and takes effort to 'relearn' (or actually, learn) after it's been lost.

The Bjorks remind us that an item in memory can be characterised by two strengths – *storage strength* (how embedded or interconnected a memory representation is with related knowledge and skills) and *retrieval strength* (how easily a memory representation can be activated or accessed when needed). They state that 'current performance is entirely a function of current retrieval strength, but that storage strength acts to retard the loss (forgetting) and enhance the gain (relearning) of retrieval strength'.

The key idea is that the conditions that most rapidly increase retrieval strength differ from those that maximise the gain of storage strength. If learners interpret current retrieval strength (performance on a test) as storage strength (learning), they're fooling themselves. They become prone to preferring poorer conditions of learning (e.g., study strategies such as cramming for a test) to better conditions of learning (e.g., testing yourself intermittently). Students feel more successful using the poorer conditions for learning while struggling under the better conditions.

The Bjorks went on a mission to figure out what these 'better conditions' are; conditions that seem to initially create difficulty but lead to more durable (i.e., improved 'storage strength'; remembering long-term) and flexible learning (i.e., improved 'retrieval strength'; being able to apply something at a later moment and/or in different contexts). These conditions are what they dubbed desirable difficulties and they describe five.

Five characteristics of desirable difficulty

Interleaving/variable practice: In interleaving, you vary the conditions of practice. You mix (i.e., interleave) practice on several related skills together. In other words, you don't block practice, repeating the same type of task over and over again but rather shuffle tasks around. For instance, a pianist, after having learned the scales and chords, will alternate practice between scales, chords, and arpeggios. A tennis player, after having acquired the skills of hitting a forehand, backhand, and volley will alternate their practice between them. After all, that is also what is needed when playing the piano or tennis.

Contextual interference: Contextual interference (doing the same thing often but in different situations or contexts) is very similar to interleaving but here you make the task environment – not the task itself – more variable or unpredictable in a way that creates a temporary interference for the learner. For instance, did you know that even studying the same material in two different rooms leads to increased recall of that material?

Spaced practice: This is also known as 'distributed practice' and is about spacing learning over time. Instead of studying for an hour and a half, you split your study into three sessions of 30 minutes with one or more days in between. Distributing practice (e.g., learning tasks, study attempts, training trials) supports long-term retention through consolidation (giving your brain the chance to let things gel) and retrieval practice (recalling what you've learned).

Reduced feedback: Reducing feedback frequency and specificity makes life more difficult for learners during training but – as with all desirable difficulties – can enhance long-term performance. It stimulates their independence, knowing that the instructor won't give them the answer in the end. Examples of 'reducing' feedback are giving summary feedback at the end of a practice session or 'fading' the frequency of feedback over sessions.

Retrieval practice/practice testing: In a nutshell, practice testing 'forces' learners to try to recall what they've previously learned from memory, usually as opposed to rereading. Because they actively remember that information – retrieve it from their memory – they can remember it better and longer.

This is what desirable difficulties are. They're about conditions that create certain types of challenges, focused on slowing the rate of apparent learning so that long-term retention and transfer are optimised.[37] The Bjorks call it 'making it difficult but in a good way'.

Unmasking the illusion

We approach breaking this illusion from three perspectives. The first is that of the teacher and how they must help students understand the difference between making learning harder and making learning harder in a good way. Making learning harder through productive failure, discovery learning, or simply setting tasks that are beyond students' grasp is not desirable because it is based upon the idea that we learn more from failure than success or that we learn better when we discover something ourselves. On the other hand, when teachers understand cognitive architecture, and how it relates to learning, they're better placed to discern the differences between desirable and undesirable difficulties.

The second deals with how teachers are often evaluated. School leaders, school inspectors, and the like must stop evaluating teachers and their teaching in terms of student performance on exams, student satisfaction, and/or self-reported judgements of learning during the lessons or at the end of the term. They need to carry out comprehensive objective analyses of real, long-term learning looking at later successes and failures in settings far removed from both the original learning and the teacher. Cumulative testing is a beginning.

The third perspective is the learner. Children and adolescents are not famed for their ability to delay gratification. As such, making the right choice between expending minimal effort to achieve short-term gratification (i.e., getting a passing grade on an exam) versus cognitively struggling a bit to achieve long-term learning can be a difficult prospect. As stated, the learner is after all a *discipulus economicus*. They're naturally going to go for the former.

Conclusion

The easy-wins illusion is challenging but not insurmountable. Addressing it requires a two-pronged attack, namely knowledge and skills on the one hand and experience on the other. By knowledge and skills, we mean the learner needs to be explicitly taught what desirable difficulties are and why they hold great utility for learning, before acquiring the skills necessary to live into that understanding.

Conversely, students need to experience that these techniques work. Through non-threatening testing situations such as low-stakes formative assessment or no-stakes testing, students see how they can achieve success without investing more time, since the only extra investment required comes in the form of mental effort.

If teachers can prove this to students, that learning slower and harder is not a bad thing, then students will be more likely to embrace the desirable side of difficulty.

6. The motivation illusion

'It is not only right to strike while the iron is hot, but that it may be very practicable to heat it by continually striking.'[38]

In 1984, Alexey Pajitnov made a remarkable discovery while designing what would become one of the most influential cultural phenomena of all time. When experimenting with algorithms and puzzles to test hardware capabilities, he was inspired by pentominoes – a mathematical puzzle involving shapes made of five squares. Pajitnov simplified the concept to tetrominoes (shapes made of four squares), creating a game that blended simplicity with endless challenge, and so *Tetris* was born.

As he developed the game at the Moscow Academy of Sciences, Pajitnov observed something unexpected about human engagement. Players remained absorbed in the experience not because they started with any particular interest in geometric puzzles, but through their growing mastery of each small challenge. Each successful block placement led naturally to the next, creating what he called a 'delicious cycle of mastery'. What began as a simple programming exercise revealed a profound truth about human learning, motivation, and achievement.

This principle emerged not just in *Tetris*, but across the nascent field of game design. When Shigeru Miyamoto created *Super Mario Bros.* in 1985, he deliberately structured the first level to ensure players experienced success within seconds. Each jump, each coin collected, each obstacle overcome built players' competence and motivation incrementally. James Paul Gee discusses how more recent games like *Portal* masterfully scaffold learning through what he calls 'pleasantly frustrating' challenges.[39] Each puzzle builds incrementally on previous solutions, creating what game designers call a 'compulsion loop' – where small achievements drive continued engagement.

What Pajitnov discovered through observation, cognitive scientists would later confirm through research. Studies on the neuroscience of learning show that achievement triggers dopaminergic responses in the brain's reward system, creating what Murayama calls a 'reward-learning framework'[40] – where success reinforces engagement. This mirrors exactly what Pajitnov observed in his players: achievement creating its own motivation.

The illusion

Many people think that motivation leads to success; that if you motivate a child, or better yet if you can achieve some state of intrinsic motivation in that child, learning will naturally follow. This sounds good and even logical, but unfortunately this causal relation of motivation leading to success (in school, success = learning) is a myth. In a landmark study tracking 1,478 children from Grades 1 to 4, Garon-Carrier and colleagues found that achievement consistently predicted subsequent motivation, but not vice versa.[41] Students who experienced success in mathematics developed greater intrinsic motivation towards maths over time, but higher motivation alone did not lead to improved achievement. Like Pajitnov's players who became increasingly engaged through mastering each level, the students' motivation grew from their experiences of competence. The researchers noted that motivation behaved as a 'developmental construct' – more malleable at the start but becoming 'progressively more crystallized through experiences of achievement'. This pattern held true regardless of gender or initial ability level, suggesting a fundamental principle about how human motivation actually works.

If there's one central message in this book, and indeed one defining characteristic of the human mechanisms of learning, it's that what we think works or is good for learning and what *actually* works or is good for learning are often some distance apart. Like many misconceptions about how we learn, there is often a grain of truth cloaked in a shroud of delusion. This is no more apparent than in how we think about the relationship between motivation and learning. There persists a belief that motivation precedes or is even a cause of achievement, but there is strong evidence that we have the causal arrow the wrong way round.

The assumption that some internal motivation sparks external achievement feels intuitive. It aligns with cultural narratives of inspiration: the student who dreams of becoming a scientist, the writer burning with passion to pen the next great novel, or the athlete who wakes at dawn driven by a love for their sport. While motivation might prompt initial engagement, it's often the act of achieving – however small – that sustains effort and fuels continued progress. This idea challenges a core assumption in education: that fostering motivation is the first step to improving performance. Instead, they suggest a shift in focus. If we want to inspire students, we must first help them succeed. Small achievements – whether solving a problem, writing a coherent paragraph, or performing a simple experiment – are the building blocks of motivation. Without these tangible successes, enthusiasm alone rarely leads to meaningful progress. Far from being an abstract precursor to learning, motivation is an outcome of the learning process itself, born of effort, competence, and the belief that success is possible. This doesn't mean we believe motivation isn't important – every teacher should strive to motivate their students. Motivation plays a key role in encouraging students to begin a task and/or learn something new, which is crucial. However, if a motivated student encounters failure early on (i.e., hits a brick wall) and doesn't experience success, their motivation will quickly fade. Conversely, when an initially 'unmotivated' student achieves success and realises they're capable of completing the task, they become motivated to continue. Success is compelling – it builds confidence and creates a desire for more. Consider two approaches to introducing essay writing.

In the success-first approach, a teacher breaks essay writing into small steps – crafting single paragraphs on familiar topics before building to complete essays. Students who initially declared 'I hate writing' find themselves engaged because they've experienced tangible success at each stage. Their motivation visibly grows with each achievement. However, in the 'brick wall' approach, students face a complex essay assignment with minimal scaffolding. Despite an initial motivational pep talk, most quickly encounter frustration. Their motivation – whatever its initial level – collapses when confronted with their perceived incompetence. By the end, many have produced little and reinforced the belief that 'I'm just not good at writing'.

One of the risks of relying too heavily on the concept of motivation is that we don't really know what it is, and this can obscure the actual mechanisms of learning. Motivation is a vague construct that often serves as a convenient explanation rather than a precise one. Educators may assume that if students are unmotivated, they need to be inspired. However, the real solution often lies in addressing their competence and providing opportunities for achievement. Graham Nuthall's research further illustrates this point. In *The Hidden Lives of Learners*,[42] Nuthall found that students are often most engaged with material they already know well. While this engagement may appear productive, it rarely leads to new learning. As we explored in the previous illusion, true progress requires grappling with what Robert and Elizabeth Bjork call 'desirable difficulties' – tasks that are mentally challenging in the short term but lead to greater long-term gains.[43]

Kou Murayama's argument that motivation may be better understood as a linguistic construct than a cognitive one is particularly relevant here.[44] According to Murayama, behaviours traditionally attributed to motivation – like striving for competence or curiosity – can often be explained by tangible mechanisms such as feedback and reward. Students appear 'motivated' when they achieve tangible successes, suggesting that motivation is an emergent property rather than a precursor to learning.

Another key aspect of this problem with the word itself is the decline in motivation over time and how important that is later on. Research consistently shows that both self-concept (students' perceptions of their own abilities) and intrinsic value (the enjoyment or importance they attach to a subject) tend to decline during the first three years of school.[45] This decline is not only a concerning trend but also a crucial insight into the role of achievement in sustaining motivation. Without consistent success in the classroom early on, students often lose confidence in their abilities and disengage from learning tasks, creating a downward spiral that can be challenging to reverse. When students achieve small, tangible victories – solving a problem, mastering a new skill, or receiving positive feedback – they develop a sense of competence and control over their learning. This competence reinforces their belief in their abilities, making them more likely to engage with future challenges. Conversely, students who struggle without experiencing success begin to question their abilities, leading to declines in both self-concept and intrinsic value. For example, a student who struggles with reading but learns to decode a challenging passage is likely to feel more competent, fostering a sense of self-efficacy. This newfound confidence becomes a foundation for further effort and engagement.

It's important to note that self-perception in the form of self-concept and efficacy is not a uniform trait but varies across domains. A student may feel confident and capable in mathematics while perceiving themselves as inadequate in history. This domain-specific nature of self-belief underscores the importance of targeted achievement-building strategies. Broad interventions aimed at fostering a 'global' sense of motivation or competence often fall short because they fail to address the specific areas where students most need support. This variability in motivation across domains calls into question the overly generalised narratives around approaches like growth mindset. While the idea that 'intelligence is malleable' has gained significant traction, its application is often too broad to be of any tangible use. Workshops on brain plasticity or inspirational stories about overcoming failure may spark temporary enthusiasm, but they rarely translate into lasting changes in behaviour. Students may adopt a growth mindset in one area while remaining fixed in another, depending on their prior experiences and perceived competence. Encouraging students to 'love learning' or 'believe in themselves' may have limited impact if they do not experience success in specific areas. Targeted strategies that build competence in particular domains – such as scaffolded instruction in maths or phonics training in reading – are far more effective at initiating the achievement-motivation cycle.

One area where this competence-confidence illusion is particularly evident is in the area of reading. Studies show that literacy skills fuel reading enjoyment, not vice versa.[46] A child who struggles to read fluently is unlikely to enjoy reading, no matter how engaging the material or how much they are encouraged to find joy in books. However, as their reading skills improve along with having the necessary background knowledge to understand/comprehend what they're reading, they begin to access more complex and rewarding texts, leading to greater enjoyment and a self-reinforcing cycle of engagement and achievement. Part of the explanation for this dynamic is in the concept of a motivation-achievement cycle. As students achieve success, they experience a sense of reward that reinforces their engagement. This cycle begins with small, tangible wins that build competence. This feedback loop challenges traditional motivational theories such as self-determination theory (SDT),[47] which posits that intrinsic motivation arises when autonomy, competence, and relatedness needs are met. While SDT emphasises the importance of competence, it assumes that motivation is a precursor to achievement. Yet studies – including longitudinal research on mathematics achievement – suggest otherwise and give strong support to the idea that achievement consistently predicts intrinsic motivation over time, not the reverse.[48]

Unmasking the illusion

To address the illusion between achievement and motivation, educators must design learning environments that take into account the often counterintuitive nature of how learning happens. Two strategies from Barak Rosenshine are helpful here in reconciling the illusion.[49] One essential strategy is presenting information in small, manageable steps (Rosenshine Principle 2). Breaking down complex tasks into smaller components reduces cognitive load in the initial states of learning, making it more likely that students will experience early successes. Equally critical is ensuring a high success rate during guided practice (Rosenshine Principle 7). His work suggests that when students are successful around 80% of the time during learning activities, they remain engaged and confident without becoming complacent. This balance helps students perceive tasks as achievable, reducing anxiety while reinforcing their belief in their own abilities. Monitoring and adjusting tasks based on student performance can help maintain this optimal level of success. Another critical component is *actionable feedback*. Contrary to common assumptions, effective feedback requires thoughtful consideration of when and how it's delivered. The timing of feedback deserves careful calibration. Indeed, research increasingly shows that delayed feedback often produces better long-term learning than immediate responses by creating retrieval challenges that enhance retention. Similarly, feedback should maintain a delicate balance: focused enough to guide improvement without becoming so specific that it merely provides a recipe for the current task rather than developing the learner's capabilities. It is not enough to simply tell students they're doing well; effective feedback identifies what they have achieved while connecting these achievements to underlying principles that transfer beyond the immediate context. This approach not only reinforces competence but also develops independent learning capabilities, bridging the gap between where students are and where they aim to be.

This particular illusion highlights a running theme in this book, which is that to achieve certain outcomes, you need to do the opposite of that outcome. It might appear to the casual observer that allowing students total freedom in how to do a task might be motivating and many tasks can indeed be 'picked up', but often this can lead to frustration when they come up against the reality of how to gain expertise in complex areas. For educators, the challenge lies in creating environments where students can achieve meaningful successes. This requires structured support, clear instruction, and actionable feedback. *Project Follow Through*, one of the most extensive educational experiments in history, provided compelling evidence that Direct Instruction (DI) not only improved academic outcomes but also positively impacted students' self-concept. Contrary to the widespread belief that explicit, structured teaching stifles creativity and intrinsic motivation, Project Follow Through demonstrated that students in DI programmes consistently outperformed their peers in both basic skills and measures of self-esteem. This finding challenges the notion that fostering self-concept requires unstructured or student-led learning environments. Instead, it suggests that tangible academic success, achieved through clear guidance, scaffolding, and consistent feedback, plays a critical role in shaping students' perceptions of their own abilities. When students master foundational skills and experience measurable progress, they develop a stronger sense of competence and confidence, which translates to higher self-concept scores.

Conclusion

The motivation illusion challenges a deeply ingrained intuition: that motivation must come first, leading to achievement, but Alexey Pajitnov's creation of *Tetris* provides a powerful metaphor for this process. Players didn't start motivated; their engagement emerged as they experienced incremental success. This same principle applies to learning: success, even in small doses, fosters motivation, creating a cycle of achievement and engagement. This insight has profound implications for education. It suggests that the most effective way to inspire students is not to focus on abstract notions of motivation but to create opportunities for tangible, incremental success. Many students have never experienced academic success, and even a small taste of this can be transformative for those students. By structuring tasks, scaffolding learning, and providing actionable feedback, educators can set the stage for meaningful achievements that build both competence and confidence.

7. The discovery illusion

> 'To try to discover by oneself what has already been discovered is a waste of time.'[50]

In 1762, Jean-Jacques Rousseau wrote a novel that would fundamentally shape educational thought for centuries. *Émile, or On Education* tells the story of a boy raised according to Rousseau's 'natural' principles, isolated from the corrupting influences of society and guided by a tutor who subtly orchestrates learning experiences while remaining largely invisible.[51] Central to Rousseau's instructional philosophy is the belief that children should discover knowledge for themselves rather than receive direct instruction: 'Let him not be taught science, let him discover it,' he famously wrote in *Émile*.

Rousseau remained remarkably faithful to his own principles, demonstrating the ultimate, and most tragic, application of his educational philosophy by abandoning his own children to the uncertainties of self-discovery. Convinced he was incapable of providing them with a proper upbringing, he placed all five of his children in the Paris Foundling Hospital between 1746 and 1752, reasoning that institutional care would serve them better than his own guidance. While we should be cautious about judging historical actions through a modern lens, this decision nonetheless exposes a glaring contradiction at the heart of his educational ideals. Historian Jean-Pierre Bardet's research on 18th-century Parisian foundling hospitals reveals that approximately two-thirds of children admitted died within their first year, with mortality rising to nearly 90% by age 10.[52] Voltaire, Rousseau's acerbic contemporary and frequent critic, seized on this hypocrisy, noting that Rousseau had written extensively on education yet 'did not even know how to raise his own children'.[53]

What Rousseau's philosophy illustrates is that there's a world of difference between appearances and reality. When we observe students engaged in what seem to be discovery activities – collaborating on a science experiment, debating interpretations of a historical document, or struggling with a mathematical problem – we see engagement, effort, and occasionally a rare moment of insight. These visible signs of student 'ownership' of the process of discovery create a compelling illusion that students are better placed to marshal their own learning than a knowledgeable and highly effective teacher. Like Rousseau's imaginary pupil Émile, these students appear to be constructing knowledge naturally and meaningfully.

The discovery illusion remains one of education's most enduring though destructive misconceptions: the belief that students' natural engagement in self-directed activities leads to structured, durable learning.

The illusion

The illusion that children learn best when they discover things for themselves positions student-led learning as enlightened practice while characterising explicit instruction as outdated or even harmful. This perspective resonates with deeply held Western cultural values of independence, creativity, and self-determination, lending it an almost moral authority in educational discourse.

The illusion takes hold when we observe students working in groups to research a new topic, providing peer-to-peer support and correcting one another's work. These visible signs of discovery create a compelling impression of learning. Yet research consistently shows that rather than developing robust understanding, students frequently reinforce misconceptions, make minimal progress despite significant effort, or engage in what Robert Coe aptly termed 'poor proxies for learning'.[54]

Several cognitive mechanisms sustain this illusion. First is the *effort fallacy* – the misconception that struggle itself indicates effective learning. When students wrestle with discovering concepts independently, the cognitive effort involved creates an illusion of understanding, regardless of whether accurate learning or understanding has occurred. This connects to the wider belief that discovery represents the most *natural* way to learn. This natural learning assumption conflates two fundamentally different types of learning. Biologically primary learning (like spoken-language acquisition) occurs naturally through environmental exposure. It has evolutionarily evolved and is critical to the survival of our species. However, virtually all academic content involves biologically secondary learning – cultural artefacts like reading, mathematics, and science – that the human brain has not evolved to acquire without structured instruction.

Confirmation bias further reinforces the illusion, as proponents selectively remember and celebrate occasional discovery success stories while overlooking or rationalising the more frequent instances of confusion and frustration. These cognitive biases combine with ideological commitments that frame discovery approaches as inherently more progressive, democratic, and emancipatory than traditional instruction.

Perhaps most fundamentally, the discovery illusion rests on a profound category error: the confusion between how experts create knowledge and how novices acquire it. While scientists and professionals make discoveries that advance knowledge in their fields, they do so by leveraging extensive existing knowledge structures. Novice learners, by definition, lack these foundations. Expecting students to learn primarily through discovery is akin to expecting someone to compose symphonies before mastering musical notation; it fundamentally misunderstands the prerequisites for meaningful discovery.

Epistemology isn't pedagogy

Derek Hodson wrote that there's a fundamental difference between scientists (experts) and students, namely that while scientists *do* science, students *learn* science.[55] The article 'Epistemology or pedagogy, that is the question' challenges the illusion that how knowledge is acquired within a discipline (its epistemology) isn't the same as how it should be taught (the instruction/pedagogy).[56] While fields like the natural and social sciences rely on discovery and experimentation, this doesn't mean that students should be taught through discovery learning. The belief that students should learn in the same way that scientists do has led to educational approaches that overlook the cognitive differences between experts and novices.[57] Instead of seeing students as learners who need structured instruction, many teachers, teacher trainers, and curriculum designers assume that students can engage in professional-level inquiry without foundational knowledge.

Unlike experts, novices – and in this respect almost all students – lack the conceptual frameworks necessary for meaningful discovery. Research on expert–novice differences in fields like chess,[58] medicine, and physics further confirms that experts operate with deeply structured knowledge, while novices rely on surface-level understanding. When students are placed in unguided discovery environments, they often fail to grasp key concepts, reinforcing misconceptions rather than developing expertise.

Finally, this idea of discovery as the way to gain knowledge mirrors outdated views of how science itself works. Scientific knowledge is not built purely through inductive observation (that 'aha moment' of insight) but also through theoretical frameworks that guide inquiry. Learners miss those frameworks. Learners need carefully structured instruction that builds their conceptual understanding before engaging in inquiry-based activities.

Our cognitive architecture

Though *minimally guided instructional* approaches such as discovery learning, problem-based learning, and inquiry-based learning are intuitively appealing, they're largely ineffective because of how human cognitive architecture functions. Working memory is very limited in its capacity (4–7 elements) and duration (3–25 seconds). This makes discovery an inefficient way to acquire new knowledge as the learner must rely on an inefficient trial-and-error approach that novices use when they lack prior knowledge or structured guidance. Instead of applying learned strategies or schemas, they rely on random exploration (John Sweller calls this the *randomness as genesis* principle[59]), which overloads working memory. Novices thus struggle when placed in discovery-based learning environments because their working memory becomes overloaded with unstructured information. As a result, discovery learning often leads to misconceptions, fragmented knowledge, and increased cognitive load without meaningful learning gains. This is in direct opposition to the *borrowing and reorganising* principle, which permits the rapid building of a long-term memory store by borrowing information from another person's long-term memory; that is, by being taught.

Despite the continued popularity of discovery learning, research overwhelmingly supports the use of structured, guided learning approaches[60] except in those rare cases where a select group of students have a high enough level of prior knowledge.[61] For the rest of us, discovery is generally inefficient.

Unmasking the illusion

If discovery approaches represent educational romanticism, then what constitutes educational realism? Evidence overwhelmingly suggests that novice learners require structured instructional techniques rather than the ineffective path of unguided discovery. This isn't to suggest self-directed learning lacks value, but that such approaches must follow established knowledge foundations.

The worked-example effect provides a powerful alternative to discovery approaches. By studying expert solutions before attempting similar problems independently, students benefit from externalising the problem-solving process, freeing cognitive resources and allowing development of robust mental models. Research consistently shows novices learn more effectively and efficiently when instruction begins with worked examples and gradually transitions to independent problem solving.

Guided practice with immediate feedback further distinguishes effective instruction from discovery approaches. Students engage in structured application of new knowledge with opportunities for correction before misconceptions become entrenched. The optimal approach maintains success rates around 80% – balancing motivation without inducing frustration or complacency. The 'I do, We do, You do' model represents a practical synthesis of these principles. Unlike discovery approaches that might begin and end with 'You do', this sequence acknowledges the fundamental role of teacher expertise. The crucial distinction lies in the preparatory phases that discovery approaches often neglect, leaving students without the knowledge necessary for meaningful inquiry.

What emerges is not a rejection of discovery's aims – intellectual autonomy and conceptual understanding – but recognition that these require structured pathways rather than premature unguided exploration. What discovery advocates miss is that true intellectual independence requires extensive guided preparation; the expert's capacity for discovery represents the culmination, not the beginning, of the learning process.

Conclusion

The illusion that learning flourishes primarily through self-directed discovery persists in spite of and not because of empirical support, because it resonates with deeply held cultural values and misapplies observations about expert cognition to novice learners. This romantic vision of education traces its lineage from Rousseau through progressive education movements to contemporary constructivist approaches, gaining strength from its alignment with ideals of creativity, autonomy, and natural development. The discovery illusion persists precisely because its surface-level manifestations – engaged students, hands-on activity, apparent effort – provide compelling theatre that masks the cognitive reality beneath.

What cognitive science reveals, however, is a fundamental mismatch between this idealised vision and the architectural constraints of human learning. Working memory limitations, the distinction between biologically primary and secondary knowledge, and the qualitative differences between expert and novice cognition all converge on a single conclusion: discovery learning represents one of the least effective, efficient, and fulfilling pathways to robust understanding for most academic content. The evidence is not marginal but overwhelming; across domains, age groups, and contexts, minimally guided approaches consistently underperform structured instruction for novice learners.

The challenges associated with the discovery illusion have profound implications for educational equity. Discovery approaches, if and when they occasionally work, often advantage students who already possess substantial background knowledge and metacognitive skills, typically those from more privileged backgrounds, while disadvantaging precisely those students most in need of explicit instruction. The romanticisation of discovery thus inadvertently perpetuates educational disparities under the guise of progressive pedagogy.

The alternative isn't a return to passive, rote instruction, but rather the implementation of instructional approaches that acknowledge both cognitive limitations and the ultimate goal of conceptual understanding. Worked examples, scaffolding, guided practice, retrieval activities, and gradual release models all provide pathways to genuine intellectual autonomy that discovery approaches promise but seldom deliver. These evidence-informed methods create the cognitive foundations upon which meaningful discovery can eventually occur. The most enlightened educational approach isn't one that romanticises discovery, but one that strategically builds towards it through evidence-informed instruction that respects both the constraints and the potential of the human mind.

8. The uniqueness illusion

'Teaching is interesting because students are so different, but it is only possible because they are so similar.'[62]

If you look at a group of people anywhere, you'll see tall and short people, younger and older people, people from all races, and mixtures thereof with different skin and hair colours, eye colours, and so forth. You'll see very athletic people and people who live more sedentary lives, very artistic people and people who can't beat a drum or draw a straight line with a ruler, and religious people who believe in one or more gods and humanists and/or atheists. But biologically speaking, we're all the same.

Consider, for instance, the digestive system. While there exist differences in metabolism, stomach size, biome, food preferences, and also potential digestive issues, we can safely say that (barring anomalies) we all digest things the same way. This is also true for our skeletal and muscular systems, respiratory systems, circulatory systems, and nervous systems including our brains.

Thus, while we're all different in a host of ways, when it comes to cognition, we're all essentially the same in biological terms – and herein lies the illusion. As humans we seek patterns to such an extent that we often locate them where they don't exist. When it comes to differences between learners, we therefore tend to assume that the cognitive supports students need are so rich and varied that they require careful mapping and attention in order to support all students according to whichever 'types of learner' we are trying to teach.

In reality, since there's so much more that makes us similar than different, teachers must work with universal aspects of our cognitive architecture while still adapting their teaching to individual differences.

The illusion

If you're a teacher or parent, you know better than most that children differ in many ways. They have different interests, learn at different speeds, have different talents, and so on. This is indisputable and means that we must take note of these differences and not try to teach all learners in exactly the same way. On the other hand, what's also indisputable is that students all learn in the same way; that is to say they all have the same cognitive architecture. Let's start with the latter.

Information processing and cognitive architecture

We all have a brain made up of nearly 100 billion nerve cells, or neurons, in two connected hemispheres. Both hemispheres have specific regions related to different cognitive and physical functions. The left hemisphere, for example, in general, has regions associated with logical tasks such as language, mathematics, and analytical thinking, while the right hemisphere generally has regions linked to creativity, spatial ability, and intuition. However, there's no such thing as being right- or left-brained, and we can't multitask.

When we process information and learn we're talking about our cognitive architecture. Human cognitive architecture refers to how our cognitive system is organised and processes information. Essentially, it's the blueprint underlying how we perceive, interpret, store, and retrieve information. This architecture consists of three interrelated and connected information stores or memories.

The first is sensory memory where information from our five senses (eyes, ears, nose, tongue, sensory nerves) is first processed. This sensory memory is very short (1–3 seconds before the information is lost). Of the millions of bits of information (stimuli) bombarding us every second, the only information that proceeds through this architecture to make the jump to our working memory is what we attend to. The name says it all; working memory is where the work happens.

Working memory is a temporary store that holds and manipulates information for complex cognitive tasks like reasoning, learning, and comprehension. It has a limited capacity of 4–7 pieces of information and thus can become easily overloaded. It also has a limited retention duration of 3–20 seconds. If you don't do anything with that information in that period such as repeat it several times as in a telephone number[63] or relate it to what you already know, it's gone. If you process that attended-to information, it then moves to long-term memory, which is limitless in capacity and duration.

Information in working memory is encoded into long-term memory for more permanent storage in ordered knowledge schemas, which become broader and deeper as new information is added (or in some cases new schemas are started and built upon), and conversely, long-term memory provides knowledge and experiences that can be retrieved and temporarily held in working memory for use in current tasks. Effective learning involves transferring information back and forth between these two stores to build lasting knowledge so we can apply it when needed.

Based upon our cognitive architecture and decades of cognitive psychological and educational research, we now have a large arsenal of instructional interventions that we can use to help our students learn and our teachers teach more effectively, efficiently, and in a more fulfilling way (that is to say, they experience success).

So, should we teach all learners in the same way?

Whenever one of the authors presents this, one of the major questions posed by someone in the audience is 'Are you saying that we all learn in the same way and that teaching is a set of techniques/tricks where one size fits all?' Voila: the illusion.

The answer to the question is a resounding 'Yes' followed by a resounding 'No'. Just as in all other human systems, we all learn in the same way. At the same time, prior knowledge and skills, aptitude, social background, mother tongue, learning disabilities, and so forth are different for all learners. Let's first go back to the digestive system. There's no one perfect diet for everyone. Some people need larger portions than others, some people need different mixtures of foods and nutrients than others, and, in extreme cases, a diet has to be completely personalised due to sicknesses and disabilities. All of the basic aspects of digestion are the same, but for a specific person, diet needs to be tailored as long as we heed the overarching processes and constraints.

In other words, the effects of proven instructional techniques with their accompanying principles (like Barak Rosenshine's principles,[64] John Sweller's cognitive load theory, which reminds us to control intrinsic load and minimise extraneous load,[65] and Richard Mayer's cognitive theory of multimedia with its 16 multimedia principles just to name a few[66]) are broadly effective and should be applied in education. However, their implementation should never take the form of a rigid checklist that applies to every student, in every lesson, every day.

The way these principles are put into practice must be adapted to individual differences. The number and type of interventions will depend on a learner's prior knowledge and aptitude, while the amount of practice needed, as well as the optimal spacing of that practice, will vary from student to student. Younger children or those with limited prior knowledge, for example, will require more support when generating self-test questions than learners with more expertise.

Moreover, task complexity – and the intrinsic cognitive load it imposes – varies depending on expertise. What is complex for a novice may be simple for an expert, just as the appropriate step size in instruction differs depending on the learner's level of understanding. Similarly, the extraneous cognitive load introduced by an instructional technique is not universal; it too depends on a learner's prior knowledge.

In short, while these instructional principles are highly effective, their application must be flexible and responsive to individual learners rather than imposed as a one-size-fits-all approach.

Unmasking the illusion

One way to address this illusion is to acknowledge that it really isn't an illusion at all. We just happen to see it as one because our cognitive architecture exists within a black box. In many other fields, in which the activity is more outwardly observable than internal, practitioners deal with this daily. The track-and-field coach has to deal with people of all shapes and sizes learning or training to run distances ranging from the 100-metre dash to the marathon. The trainer will use the same basic principles (weight training, running intervals, varying distances, and the like) because we're all essentially the same.

Yet within that sameness, we all differ. We all need to exert strenuous effort and then rest (spaced practice) but the periods of exertion and rest will vary per discipline and athlete. We all need to vary or interleave our training (e.g., the short-distance runner will train longer distances and the marathon runner will run intervals and sprints), but here too each athlete and discipline is tailored to the situation.

Teachers also need to do this. They need to adapt proven general principles to groups of learners or even individual learners. If we take Rosenshine's 10 principles of instruction as an example and only look at younger (primary or elementary school) versus older (secondary or high school) learners, this might mean:

1. **Begin a lesson with a short review of previous learning:** For younger learners, use 'fun' activities like songs, games, or quick

questions. For older learners, use more structured reviews, such as quizzes or discussions that link past lessons to new material.

2. **Present new material in small steps with learner practice after each step:** For younger learners, break down complex ideas using stories, visuals, or hands-on activities. For older learners, give step-by-step explanations and use visual aids like outlines or graphic organisers.

3. **Ask a large number of questions and check the responses of all learners:** With younger learners, use open-ended questions to spark curiosity, giving them time to think. For older learners, ask deeper, more epistemic questions like 'How?' and 'Why?' and encourage discussions among peers.

4. **Provide models:** For younger learners, use relatable examples like physical demonstrations or drawings. For older learners, show worked examples, detailed walkthroughs, or abstract models like formulas. For both groups, be the model yourself!

5. **Guide learner practice:** For young learners provide immediate feedback through guided practice activities like group work or hands-on tasks. For older learners delay feedback and use more independent practice with monitoring through formative assessments.

6. **Check for learner understanding:** With younger learners, do quick checks like thumbs up/down, mini-whiteboards, or 'show-and-tell' moments. For older learners, use quizzes, paired discussions, or short written responses.

7. **Obtain a high success rate:** Give younger learners tasks that are challenging yet achievable. You might want to use games or rewards to motivate. For older learners, use different levels of tasks so they experience success but are still pushed to improve.

8. **Provide scaffolds for difficult tasks:** Younger learners might need hands-on tools, guided questions, or visual aids. For older learners, offer temporary supports like templates or outlines, which can be gradually removed as they gain skills.

9. **Require and monitor independent practice:** For younger learners, give short, engaging tasks with lots of feedback. For older learners, assign longer, self-paced activities and help them monitor their progress.

10. **Engage learners in weekly and monthly review:** Use cumulative activities for younger learners, like storytelling, drawings, or group projects. For older learners, reinforce learning with regular quizzes,

comprehensive exams, or reflective journalling to improve retention over time.

By adapting Rosenshine's principles to different ages, aptitudes, learning needs, learning challenges, and so forth, teachers can create a supportive and challenging learning environment that maximises the potential for all learners to succeed.

In other words, one size definitely doesn't fit all.

Conclusion

The uniqueness illusion is pervasive because it relies on a basic human premise: all people are special and unique. Though this is undeniably true, as educators we also need to acknowledge that (at least in cognitive terms) our students are more similar than we might first think – since the illusion only works because we believe we ought to choose between the two. In reality, if educators can hold the universal nature of cognitive architecture *and* individual student differences at the same time, we stand to make better, more nuanced choices on behalf of *all* learners.

9. The performance illusion

'We may feel we have learned something simply because it is fresh in mind, but that feeling is fleeting.'[67]

In early 1900s Berlin, a horse named Hans stunned audiences by seemingly displaying human-level intelligence. Owned by Wilhelm von Osten, a mathematics teacher and amateur scientist, Hans seemingly solved mathematical problems and recognised written words. A typical feat would involve von Osten asking Hans a maths question, such as 'What is 3 + 4?', at which point Hans would respond by tapping his hoof seven times. Scientists, educators, and even the German Board of Education were floored, as Hans' responses were accurate an astonishing 89% of the time.[68]

Experts far and wide were convinced of Hans' mathematical ability until psychologist Oskar Pfungst noticed something no one else had the eyes to see. He realised Hans was not doing mathematics at all, but was instead responding to subtle, unconscious cues from his questioners. When someone posed a problem, they would involuntarily tense up as Hans approached the correct number of taps. Once Hans reached the correct answer, the questioner would subtly relax – often by a slight movement of the head, change in posture, or breath adjustment – which signalled Hans to stop tapping.

Though we are not suggesting human learners are akin to a foot-tapping horse, there is nevertheless a worthwhile comparison to draw: just as Hans' performances created an illusion of understanding, students' classroom performances can create similar illusions of learning that mask what's really happening beneath the surface.

Here we will discuss these two seemingly synonymous but very different educational terms, as well as revealing a pervasive illusion at the centre: that certain teaching and learning strategies that are beneficial for performance aren't good for, and can even impede, learning.

The illusion

To address this illusion, we first need to define performance and learning in accurate terms. What we teach may go into our students' memory, and during or directly after instruction they may be able to discuss ideas with classmates, answer questions, and even do their homework. But it isn't learning if nothing is retained and what was taught can't be recalled and used next week, month, or year. Nick Soderstrom and Robert Bjork write:

> The primary goal of instruction should be to facilitate long-term learning—that is, to create relatively permanent changes in comprehension, understanding, and skills of the types that will support long-term retention and transfer. During the instruction or training process, however, what we can observe and measure is performance, which is often an unreliable index of whether the relatively long-term changes that constitute learning have taken place.[69]

Performance, therefore, is a short-term change in one's knowledge or, as Soderstrom and Bjork say, 'Temporary fluctuations in behavior or knowledge that can be observed and measured during or immediately after the acquisition process.' Some researchers refer to this as intermediate-term memory, lasting little more than a few hours. A student might remember it during or shortly after a lesson, but it's usually quickly forgotten. For instance, how many of you reading this have taught something and even administered a test that your students passed, only to find that after the weekend, they look at you with blank stares when you mention it? In other words, the knowledge gained is *fragile*. It's easily disrupted, error-prone, and quickly forgotten. With respect to performance, relearning is actually reacquisition. It takes almost as long to reacquire the lost knowledge as it was to acquire it the first time, and if that reacquisition occurs after a substantial period, you might even question whether you had actually 'learned' it at all.

Learning, on the other hand, is defined by one of the authors as a change in long-term memory;[70] enduring changes in knowledge, skills, and behaviour for long-term retention and transfer. Learning is stable; what you've learned deeply and durably isn't easily forgotten (see Table 9.1).

9. The performance illusion

Performance	Learning
• Short-term change in knowledge	• Change in long-term memory
• Fragile	• Stable
• Little/shallow cognitive information processing	• Much/deep cognitive information processing
• Fragmentary	• Cumulative
• Easily observed and measured	• Must be derived from something else

Table 9.1 Performance versus learning.

Of course, you can't always remember *everything* you've learned, but traces of it reside somewhere there in your long-term memory. To paraphrase Alfred, Lord Tennyson: ''Tis better to have learned and lost than never to have learned at all.'[71] This means that though you might not remember it, 'relearning' it goes much more quickly than learning it the first time.

Take riding a bicycle, for instance. If you haven't ridden a bike in 20 or 30 years, you'll be very shaky and will probably fall when you first get back on. However, within a short time – a lot shorter than it took to learn to ride the bike in the first place – you're again able to ride fairly proficiently.

> Paul's grandfather Jack had become senile and as he was nearing death, he began saying things that nobody understood. At a certain point, someone ascertained that he was singing Russian nursery rhymes and speaking Russian. Grandpa Jack was born in Odessa (now in Ukraine) and emigrated to the US when he was very young. Paul never heard him speak Russian and he had no accent. Grandpa Jack couldn't remember the rhymes but they were still there in his long-term memory. He hadn't forgotten them.

Performance requires *very little cognitive processing* and this processing is also shallow.[72] Often, performance requires nothing more than simple repetition or rehearsal in your working memory. Think of what happens when someone tells you their telephone number. You might repeat it a few times and remember it directly after hearing it, but the chance is slim that you'll remember it that evening or tomorrow. You've not processed the information in a meaningful way, and thus it doesn't get integrated into the knowledge schemas in your long-term memory.

Shallow information processing involves a minimal level of cognitive engagement. Simply repeating or rehearsing information – often without trying to understand its meaning – doesn't lead to deeper connections or integration of the information into existing knowledge structures.

Learning, on the other hand, involves *deep processing* activities like elaboration, reorganisation, and critical thinking. This meaningful and active engagement with the to-be-learned information leads to better comprehension and long-term retention. It requires a lot of cognitive/mental effort to actively process, analyse, and synthesise information; to understand the new information by relating it to prior knowledge (schema acquisition and elaboration) or by applying it in new contexts (transfer).

In short, shallow learning through rehearsal and repetition focuses on memorisation without deep comprehension, while deep learning emphasises understanding, integration, and application, leading to more effective and enduring mastery of the material.

Performance is *fragmentary*. It focuses on memorising discrete facts or pieces (fragments) of information without understanding how they relate to each other or prior knowledge. It also involves processing surface-level details such as definitions, isolated dates, or formulas where the information isn't connected to broader concepts or patterns. This makes the learning process disjointed and compartmentalised.[73]

Learning, on the other hand, is *cumulative*. It emphasises connecting new information to prior knowledge such that each new piece of learning builds on what has already been learned. This is a cumulative process that strengthens understanding and retention because the learner continuously links new ideas to existing schemas in long-term memory leading to richer, more interconnected knowledge structures.

In short, shallow learning treats information as isolated fragments rather than as part of a connected whole, while deep learning is cumulative because it builds upon existing knowledge, forming coherent and integrated schemas.

Finally, and this is probably the biggest problem with teaching for learning, is that performance is *easy to see and measure* while learning isn't. All you need to measure performance is a test or exam at the end of a week or unit. Students cram the night before, 'learn' it, and then regurgitate it.

Learning, on the other hand, is difficult to measure and needs to be delayed, derived from other things, and measured in combination with other learning. To measure learning you need to cumulatively test and/or use measures that involve analysis, synthesis, and evaluation (sorry for using Bloom's taxonomy here, but it helps). In other words, learning implies mastery and measuring true mastery is complex, time-consuming, and often subjective.

We're by no means saying that performance is bad or that it shouldn't be measured. What we're saying is that performance and learning shouldn't be confused and that the ultimate goal of teaching should be to ensure that students learn. You want what you've taught to be remembered, retrieved when needed, and applied in familiar and new situations (transfer).

Unmasking the illusion

Just as skilled illusionists can spot the telltale movements of an amateur's sleight of hand, expert teachers develop a refined ability to distinguish between the illusion of performance and genuine learning. This expertise isn't mystical – it's a carefully honed set of observational skills and diagnostic techniques.

Luckily, we as teachers have an arsenal of instructional techniques that we can use to stimulate learning. The two most well-known and effective sets of techniques are *desirable difficulties*[74] and *generative learning strategies*.[75]

As we have already explored, desirable difficulties are learning (or study) strategies that make the process of learning more challenging, but ultimately enhance long-term retention and understanding.[76] Elizabeth and Robert Bjork call this 'making things hard on yourself, but in a good way'. Although the strategies can feel frustrating or slow during study, these difficulties encourage deep processing, leading to better retention and transfer in the long run. The concept itself is counterintuitive: making learning harder in specific ways can actually improve how well we learn and retain information.

Generative learning strategies are instructional techniques that engage learners in actively constructing their understanding of new information. The Flemish use the term *herkneden* (re-knead) as in a lump of clay that can be re-kneaded or reshaped into something else. Learners use these strategies to make sense of new information, integrate it with prior knowledge, and generate new mental representations by transforming the information into something else. This encourages and requires deeper cognitive processing, leading to better comprehension and retention. Fiorella and Mayer's eight generative strategies are:

- **Summarising:** Condensing information into a brief, coherent summary.
- **Mapping:** Creating visual representations of the relationships between concepts.
- **Drawing:** Creating drawings or illustrations representing the information being learned.
- **Self-explanation:** Explaining the material to oneself as if teaching it.
- **Teaching others:** Teaching or explaining concepts to others, real or imaginary.
- **Generating questions:** Having learners create their own questions about the material.
- **Imagining:** Mentally visualising concepts or scenarios related to the material.
- **Enacting:** Acting out or physically demonstrating concepts.

Generative learning activities supersede shallow performance demonstrations because they require deep, effortful cognitive processes such as selecting relevant information, organising it into coherent representations, and integrating it with prior knowledge.

It's worth noting that students on the whole are predisposed to seeing performance as 'the main event' and learning as a necessary evil for performance. As teachers, we therefore owe it to our students to demonstrate (through approaches like generative learning strategies) that even though the road to real learning is more strenuous, it beats the fleeting nature of performance every time.

Conclusion

The lessons of this chapter invite us to reconsider the phrase: 'It's just like riding a bike.' On the one hand, we now know that the meaning behind the adage is not entirely true. After all, returning to something already learned doesn't result in instantaneous proficiency. Nevertheless, the sentiment is partially accurate in that remembering how to ride a bike comes easier than if you had never learned to in the first place.

This reveals to us the true difference between performance and learning: not only does one not equal the other, but focusing on the fragile, fragmentary nature of performance only serves to undermine durable, authentic learning.

Thankfully, unravelling this illusion is difficult but not impossible. Just ask Oskar Pfungst, who was able to solve the dilemma of Hans the mathematical horse in one simple step: he placed a blindfold over Hans' eyes.

10. The innovation illusion

'Beware of false knowledge; it is more dangerous than ignorance.'[77]

In 1985, with great fanfare, the Coca-Cola Company made what would soon be regarded as one of the greatest marketing blunders in corporate history. After spending $4 million on secretive research and conducting over 200,000 taste tests, Coca-Cola announced that it was replacing its century-old formula with 'New Coke'; a sweeter version that had consistently outperformed the original in blind taste tests. The company's leadership was convinced they were making a rational, data-driven decision. Their extensive market research showed consumers preferred the new flavour. Focus groups supported the change. The numbers were unequivocal. Roberto Goizueta, the company's chairman, boldly declared it 'the surest move ever made'.

Within days, the backlash was fierce and overwhelming. Consumers hoarded cases of the original formula. Protest groups formed across the country. The company received over 400,000 angry letters and phone calls. What Coca-Cola's sophisticated research had failed to capture was the deep emotional connection people had with the original product. The formula was not just a beverage; it had become a cultural touchstone, a symbol of tradition and nostalgia that transcended mere taste. Just 79 days after the launch of New Coke, the company was forced to reintroduce the original formula as 'Coca-Cola Classic'. During the announcement, company president Donald Keough admitted, 'We did not understand the deep emotions of so many of our customers for Coca-Cola.'[78]

The New Coke fiasco stands as a powerful metaphor for what happens when innovation is pursued without adequate consideration of contextual factors, cultural meaning, and stakeholder commitment. Coca-Cola executed what appeared to be a perfect innovation process; defining the problem (declining market share), conducting extensive research, developing a solution based on empirical evidence, and implementing it with confidence. Yet they miscalculated spectacularly by focusing exclusively on taste while overlooking the emotional and cultural significance of their product.

In education, we see the same pattern play out repeatedly, where the appeal of novelty and seemingly revolutionary approaches often overshadows the proven effectiveness of established practices. This episode reveals a profound truth about innovation: even with extensive research, resources, and expertise, the allure of the new can blind us to the value of the established. Coca-Cola executives, convinced they had found something demonstrably 'better', failed to recognise that improvement is not always about changing formulas but about understanding what truly matters to those they serve.

The illusion

The innovation illusion represents one of education's most persistent and costly misconceptions: the belief that newer teaching methods or initiatives are inherently better than established practices and that educational progress requires constant reinvention. This illusion manifests in the eager adoption of new instructional approaches, frameworks, and instructional initiatives at a policy, leadership, and classroom level before their effectiveness has been thoroughly evaluated.

The allure of this illusion is powerful for several reasons. Innovation suggests progress – and who would oppose progress? New approaches often come in the form of *solutionism*; a solution in search of a problem or a promise to solve persistent educational challenges, offering hope where previous methods may have fallen short. For teachers and administrators, embracing innovation signals forward-thinking leadership and a commitment to improvement. For policymakers and stakeholders, it demonstrates action and responsiveness to educational concerns. And above all, it's 'new'.

The cycle typically unfolds in predictable stages. First, a new approach emerges, often with a catchy name and compelling narrative. It may be grounded in legitimate research but frequently involves oversimplified interpretations of complex findings. The innovation spreads through professional conferences, social media, and professional development sessions, gaining momentum as early adopters share promising anecdotes. Schools invest significant resources in training, materials, and implementation. Teachers are encouraged or required to integrate the new approach into their practice, which often means adapting their teaching to the innovation instead of adopting the innovation into their teaching, often with limited time for mastery. When results don't match the promised transformation, the innovation is either abandoned, blamed on the teacher, or – more commonly – replaced by the next promising approach.

Consider the trajectory of educational buzzwords over recent decades: open classrooms, multiple intelligences, brain-based learning, learning styles, 21st-century skills, growth mindset, grit, personalised learning, and numerous others. Each contained elements of value but was often implemented with unrealistic expectations and insufficient attention to evidence. As Larry Cuban has documented, many of these innovations follow a predictable cycle of 'exhilaration, scientific credibility, popularity, disillusionment, and eventual decline'.[79]

The open classroom movement

The open classroom movement of the late 1960s and early 1970s emerged from a broader concept of 'open education', which included a set of assumptions derived from constructivist thought. Inspired by open office workspaces and championed by educational theorists, the movement called for removing walls between classrooms to create large, flexible spaces where students could move freely between different learning areas based on their interests. By 1970, over 10,000 American schools had adopted some version of the open classroom model, representing one of the fastest-spreading innovations in educational history.

The research increasingly shows open-plan classrooms negatively impact student learning and teacher wellbeing. A 2023 University of Melbourne study found 65% of children developed literacy faster in enclosed classrooms, with those having poor speech perception or weak attention skills suffering most in open environments.[80] Despite this evidence, educational systems like New Zealand's invested heavily in 'innovative learning environments' featuring flexible seating and removable walls. These spaces create visual, aural, and social challenges that impede focus and learning. Groovy approaches promoting 'defronted' classrooms lack sufficient evidence, noting that architectural trends like 'learning plazas' and 'agile spaces' constitute an eye-wateringly expensive grand experiment imposed without empirical justification. Educational spending should instead be guided by robust evidence across multiple outcomes.

But the detrimental impact of open-plan spaces on students is not just in terms of academic performance; it can also have a negative effect on pupil wellbeing and mental health. Excessive noise in open-plan classrooms has contributed to stress and fatigue among students, with particular impact on vulnerable students who may already have attention or auditory processing difficulties.[81] And it's not just students who are disadvantaged by open-plan, noisy environments. The teachers' health and wellbeing is also adversely affected.[82]

The rise and fall of open classrooms illustrates how educational innovations can be driven more by ideological appeal than by evidence of effectiveness. As Larry Cuban noted, 'Open space came to be seen as the physical embodiment of an educational philosophy. The architectural innovation became confused with a pedagogical innovation.'[83]

The whole language approach

The whole language approach to reading instruction offers another cautionary tale.[84] In the 1980s and 1990s, this movement swept through literacy education, promising a more natural, meaning-centred approach to reading. Traditional *phonics instruction* was dismissed as outdated and mechanical. School districts nationwide embraced whole language, revamping curricula and teacher training. California's 1987 English-Language Arts Framework explicitly endorsed whole language approaches while de-emphasising systematic phonics instruction.

The movement was compelling because it framed reading as a natural, holistic process similar to learning spoken language. It positioned teachers as facilitators rather than directors of learning and promised to make reading more engaging and meaningful for children. However, subsequent research, particularly the National Reading Panel's findings in 2000, demonstrated that systematic phonics instruction is essential for many children learning to read. The wholesale adoption of whole language without sufficient evidence led to declining reading achievement scores in California and elsewhere, eventually requiring a painful return to phonics-based approaches.

The shift from whole language to balanced literacy (and more recently, back towards structured literacy approaches) demonstrates how pendulum swings in educational practice can occur when innovations are adopted on philosophical grounds without sufficient evidence of effectiveness.

Multiple intelligences theory

Howard Gardner's theory of multiple intelligences, first proposed in 1983,[85] exemplifies how a legitimate academic theory can be transformed into an oversimplified educational movement. Gardner's idea that intelligence encompasses more than verbal-linguistic and logical-mathematical abilities was intellectually compelling and challenged the narrow conception of intelligence measured by traditional IQ tests.

Within a decade, schools across the country had enthusiastically embraced multiple intelligences theory, often in ways that went far beyond Gardner's original claims. Teachers created 'learning stations' for each intelligence, schools designed curricula around the eight intelligences, and students were assessed and sometimes even sorted according to their 'intelligence profile'. Gardner himself expressed concern about these applications, noting that 'the theory has been misused, misrepresented, and oversimplified'.[86]

The rapid adoption of multiple intelligences in education illustrates how theories originating in academia can be transformed into educational methodologies without adequate translation or testing. While Gardner's theory offered valuable insights about human cognitive capacity, the educational practices derived from it lacked empirical support.

A matter of implementation

One of the most persistent aspects of the innovation illusion is what researchers call the 'implementation gap', the gulf between how an innovation is designed and how it actually functions in everyday classroom settings.[87] Educational innovations often show promise in controlled research environments or pilot programmes with specially trained teachers, extra finances and time, and so forth but fail to deliver similar results when implemented at scale without those extras. This implementation gap has several key causes.

When schools attempt to implement new approaches quickly or without adequate resources, teachers often adopt the surface features of an innovation while maintaining their underlying practices. As Richard Elmore observed, 'Innovations that require large changes in the core of educational practice seldom penetrate more than a small fraction of classrooms.'[88] Teachers might use new terminology or rearrange their classrooms without fundamentally changing their instructional approach.

Many educational innovations require substantial shifts in teacher knowledge, skills, and beliefs. Yet professional development to support these innovations is often limited to brief workshops or training sessions with little follow-up support. Research consistently shows that meaningful instructional change requires extended professional learning opportunities with coaching, feedback, and time for practice and reflection.[89]

Innovations developed in one context often struggle when transplanted to different settings with different student populations, resources, and constraints. School culture, demographics, leadership, community expectations, and existing practices all influence how innovations are interpreted and implemented. The rapid succession of new initiatives in many school systems creates what researcher William Schmidt calls 'innovation without change'.[90] Before one approach can be fully implemented and evaluated, attention shifts to the next promising idea. This constant churn prevents deep implementation and creates reform fatigue among educators.

Unmasking the illusion

While the history of educational innovation offers plenty of reasons for scepticism, there are signs that the current movement towards evidence-informed practice might represent a more sustainable approach to educational improvement. Unlike many past innovations that promoted specific methods or approaches, evidence-informed practice is meta-innovation – a systematic way of evaluating and implementing educational changes, which adopts a laboratory to classroom approach, constantly scaling up from a controlled setting to a real-life one.

The evidence-informed practice movement emphasises critical evaluation of research evidence before adoption, ensuring contextual fit between innovations and local needs, paying careful attention to implementation quality, systematically monitoring impacts, and pursuing incremental improvement rather than wholesale change. This comprehensive approach creates a framework for educational decision making that balances rigour with practicality, helping educators distinguish between genuinely effective innovations and those that merely appear promising on the surface. Organisations like the Education Endowment Foundation in the UK and the What Works Clearinghouse in the US have developed frameworks for evaluating educational research evidence and translating it into practical guidance.

These resources help educators distinguish between practices with strong empirical support and those based primarily on theory or anecdote.

To address the innovation illusion, we must first recognise that educational improvement rarely comes from wholesale replacement of existing practices, but rather from thoughtful refinement based on evidence. This means defining a real problem, looking at the current situation and determining what's going well and what needs to be changed, and then only improving that which needs to be changed. Effective teaching practices have more commonalities than differences across generations, and many 'revolutionary' approaches repackage fundamental principles that effective teachers have long employed. In that respect, historical perspective is essential in breaking this illusion.

Conclusion

Many supposed innovations have historical antecedents, and understanding these historical cycles helps educators recognise when an innovation represents genuine advancement versus a mere rebranding of existing ideas. For example, discovery learning approaches criticised in the early 1980s reappeared under different names like 'problem-based learning' and 'inquiry learning' in subsequent decades, as Richard Mayer noted.[91] Progressive education movements from the early 20th century share remarkable similarities with 21st-century 'student-centred' approaches, while behaviourist principles from mid-century reappear in 'personalised' digital learning platforms. When we trace these genealogies of educational thought, we can better distinguish between substantive pedagogical evolution and mere terminological shifts.

The most effective educational systems maintain balance between innovation and stability. They identify core instructional practices with strong evidence of effectiveness – explicit instruction, retrieval practice, spaced learning, worked examples – and ensure these form the foundation of teaching. They pursue innovation strategically, testing new approaches through small-scale pilots with careful measurement before broader implementation.[92] They recognise that implementation quality often matters more than the specific approach.

This balanced approach might be called *disciplined innovation* – a process that embraces new possibilities while subjecting them to rigorous scrutiny. Disciplined innovation requires both openness to new ideas and scepticism about extravagant claims. It values both creativity and precision, both vision and evidence. A useful heuristic in confronting the innovation illusion is Daniel Willingham's 'strip it and flip it' framework, which offers a systematic approach to cut through the hype.[93] 'Strip it' removes emotional language to clarify what's actually being claimed; 'flip it' examines both benefits and potential drawbacks; 'trace it' investigates the innovation's origins and developers; and 'analyze it' evaluates the evidence base in your specific context. This structured scepticism helps educators move beyond the allure of novelty to focus resources on innovations with genuine potential for improving teaching and learning.

The New Coke story that opened this chapter reminds us that even the most data-driven innovations can fail when they ignore cultural context, emotional connections, and implementation realities. In education, as in business, the pursuit of novelty for its own sake often leads to disappointment and wasted resources.

Conclusion

> 'No matter how smart or well-educated you are,
> you can be deceived.'[94]

In 1973, famed illusionist and self-proclaimed psychic Uri Geller was set to appear on *The Tonight Show* with Johnny Carson. Geller's intention was to demonstrate his abilities (in the form of spoon bending, psychic powers, and telekinesis) to a mass audience in the hope that it would convince naysayers that psychic powers such as his were real.

What Uri Geller didn't account for was that Johnny Carson always did his homework on upcoming guests. A keen amateur magician himself, Carson was sceptical enough to recruit a certain James Randi (also known as The Amazing Randi) to help him figure out what Geller was up to.

Randi's approach was fundamentally scientific in nature. He began by suggesting that Carson control the conditions of the illusion. That is to say, instead of allowing Geller to bring his own props, the show provided all materials and ensured they had not been tampered with.

The result? Geller's famed psychic abilities disappeared, almost as if by magic. He failed to bend spoons or read minds, ultimately resorting to the excuse that he was feeling pressured by live television and that his energy was thrown off as a result. In reality, The Amazing Randi had exposed the illusion entirely: he worked out that Geller's spoon bending was done using pre-weakened metal combined with subtle hand movements, and how his supposed mind-reading relied on subtle suggestion techniques. The eventual impact was that millions of viewers saw Geller fail, raising unprecedented doubts about his psychic claims.

Yet Randi wasn't done there. In 1975, he wrote *The Magic of Uri Geller*,[95] explaining that all of Geller's feats could be performed using classic sleight of hand and misdirection. He then established the *James Randi Educational Foundation*[96] (JREF), which offered a $1 million prize to anyone who could demonstrate paranormal abilities under controlled conditions (no one ever won that money).

James Randi's work to expose modern-day Wizards of Oz like Uri Geller reveals to us an important truth: if illusions rely on masking us from the reality of things, that means illusions can be *un*masked. The tools of Randi's trade didn't peddle in language of illusion but rather adopted scientific norms and structures to expose the truth. In this regard, the science of learning provides educators with a similar tool.

Indeed the science of learning is *not* an initiative. It's a lens through which we see ours and others' teaching practice, as well as a means for improving that practice. Like the exposing of an illusion, understanding how learning really happens gives us the eyes to see what works, what doesn't, and what *appears* to work but doesn't.

As such, we began this book by exploring what makes an illusion. We dug into the relationship between magic and cognition, showing how illusions only work because humans are cognitively predisposed to being deceived. We then turned to education as our case in point, arguing that teaching is particularly illusory since so much of what happens when we learn is concealed from view. We then delved into 10 such illusions, examining how they came to be, before using an evidentiary lens to expose the truth of the matter.

Why is committing to this work important? Because Uri Geller himself went on to enjoy many more decades as a successful, self-proclaimed psychic. People apparently can't help but be fooled. In other words, just because we expose the illusion doesn't mean it won't come back to haunt us. The forces that drive instructional illusions aren't going anywhere. Their power will continue to be felt, to the detriment of teachers and students, unless we collectively commit to lifting the veil.

We hope this book contributes in some small way to doing just that.

Endnotes

1 The Westcar Papyrus is an ancient Egyptian text containing five stories about miracles performed by priests and magicians told at the royal court of King Khufu (Cheops) (Fourth Dynasty, 26th century BCE) by his sons.

2 Macknik, S. L., Martinez-Conde, S., & Blakeslee, S. (2010). *Sleights of mind: What the neuroscience of magic reveals about our everyday deceptions.* Henry Holt & Co.

3 Coe, R. (2013). *Improving Education: A triumph of hope over experience.* Inaugural Lecture of Professor Robert Coe, Durham University, 18 June 2013.

4 Cuban, L. (2023). *Larry Cuban on school reform and classroom practice.* Wordpress. https://larrycuban.wordpress.com/2023/12/

5 Phillpotts, E. (1918). *A shadow passes* (p. 19). Cecil Palmer & Hayward.

6 Nuthall, G. (2007). *The hidden lives of learners.* NZCER Press.

7 Tricot, A., & Sweller, J. (2014). Domain-specific knowledge and why teaching generic skills does not work. *Educational Psychology Review*, 26(2), 265–283.

8 Soderstrom, N. C., & Bjork, R. A. (2015). Learning versus performance: An integrative review. *Perspectives on Psychological Science*, 10(2), 176–199.

9 Coe, R. (2013). *Improving education: A triumph of hope over experience.* Centre for Evaluation and Monitoring.

10 Rumsfeld, D. (2002). *Defense department briefing.* Usinfo. https://usinfo.org/wf-archive/2002/020212/epf202.htm

11 Ross, L., & Ward, A. (1995). *Naive realism: Implications for social conflict and misunderstanding.* Stanford Center on Conflict and Negotiation Crown Quadrangle, (48), 103–135.

12 Kruger, J., & Dunning, D. (1999). Unskilled and unaware of it: How difficulties in recognizing one's own incompetence lead to inflated self-assessments. *Journal of Personality and Social Psychology*, 77(6), 1121–1134.

13 Gehlbach, H., Robinson, C. D., & Fletcher, A. (2024). The illusion of information adequacy. *PLOS ONE*, 19(10), e0310216.

14   Nickerson, R. S. (1999). How we know – and sometimes misjudge – what others know: Imputing one's own knowledge to others. *Psychological Bulletin*, 125(6), 737–759.

15   Tullis, J. G., & Feder, B. (2023). The 'curse of knowledge' when predicting others' knowledge. *Memory & Cognition*, 51(5), 1214–1234.

16   Clark, R. E., Feldon, D., van Merriënboer, J., Yates, K., & Early, S. (2007). Cognitive task analysis. In J. M. Spector, M. D. Merrill, J. J. G. van Merriënboer, & M. P. Driscoll (Eds.), *Handbook of research on educational communications and technology* (3rd ed.). Lawrence Erlbaum Associates. Available at: www.researchgate.net/publication/294699964_Cognitive_task_analysis

17   Grossman, A., Moore Johnson, S., & Brookover, E. (2011). *Baltimore city public schools: Implementing bounded autonomy*. PELP Case Study. PEL-063.

18   Ford, H., & Crowther, S. (1922). *My life and work*. Doubleday, Page & Co.

19   Brophy, J., & Good, T. (1986). Teacher behavior and student achievement. In M. C. Wittrock (Ed.), *Handbook of research on teaching* (3rd ed.). McMillan.

20   Bransford, J. D., Brown, A. L., & Cocking, R. R. (2000). *How people learn: Brain, mind, experience, and school*. National Academy Press.

21   Ericsson, K. A. (2006). The influence of experience and deliberate practice on the development of superior expert performance. In K. A. Ericsson, N. Charness, P. J. Feltovich, & R. R. Hoffman (Eds.), *The Cambridge handbook of expertise and expert performance* (pp. 683–703). Cambridge University Press.

22   Schön, D. A. (1983). *The reflective practitioner: How professionals think in action*. Basic Books.

23   Sweller, J., Ayres, P., & Kalyuga, S. (2011). *Cognitive load theory*. Springer.

24   Aristotle. (1995). *Categories*. Translated by J. L. Ackrill. Clarendon Press. (Original work published ca. 350 BCE.)

25   Gentner, D. (1983). Structure-mapping: A theoretical framework for analogy. *Cognitive Science*, 7(2), 155–170.

26   Thorndike, E. L., & Woodworth, R. S. (1901). The influence of improvement in one mental function upon the efficiency of other functions. *Psychological Review*, 8(3), 247–261.

27   Roediger, H. L. (1990). Implicit memory: Retention without remembering. *American Psychologist*, 45(9), 1043–1056.

28 Perkins, D. N., & Salomon, G. (1988). Teaching for transfer. *Educational Leadership*, 46(1), 22–32.

29 Lave, J., & Wenger, E. (1991). *Situated learning: Legitimate peripheral participation*. Cambridge University Press.

30 Hatano, G., & Inagaki, K. (1986). Two courses of expertise. In H. Stevenson, H. Azuma, & K. Hakuta (Eds.), *Child development and education in Japan* (pp. 262–272). W. H. Freeman.

31 Brown, A. L., & Campione, J. C. (1996). Psychological theory and the design of innovative learning environments: On procedures, principles, and systems. In L. Schauble & R. Glaser (Eds.), *Innovations in learning: New environments for education* (pp. 289–325). Lawrence Erlbaum Associates.

32 Thomas Fuller popularised this quote. He was an English churchman and historian (19 June 1608–16 August 1661).

33 Starr, R. (1971). *It don't come easy* [Song]. Apple.

34 https://www.kirschnered.nl/2022/11/09/discipulus-economicus-the-calculating-learner/

35 Bjork, E. L., & Bjork, R. A. (2011). Making things hard on yourself, but in a good way: Creating desirable difficulties to enhance learning. *Psychology and the real world: Essays illustrating fundamental contributions to society*, 2, 59–68.

36 Kirschner, P. A., Sweller, J., & Clark, R. (2006). Why minimal guidance during instruction does not work: An analysis of the failure of constructivist, discovery, problem-based, experiential, and inquiry-based teaching. *Educational Psychologist*, 41(2), 75–86.

37 Bjork, R. A., & Bjork, E. L. (2020). Desirable difficulties in theory and practice. *Journal of Applied Research in Memory and Cognition*, 9(4), 475–479.

38 Though often attributed to William Butler Yeats, the earliest known instance of this sentiment appears in a 1782 letter from Benjamin Franklin to Reverend Richard Price.

39 Gee, J. P. (2004) Learning by design: Games as learning machines. *Interactive Educational Multimedia*, 8, 15–23.

40 Murayama, K. (2022). A reward-learning framework of knowledge acquisition: An integrated account of curiosity, interest, and intrinsic–extrinsic rewards. *Psychological Review*, 129(1), 175–198.

41 Garon-Carrier, G., et al. (2016) Intrinsic motivation and achievement in mathematics in elementary school: A longitudinal investigation of their association. *Child Development*, 87(1), 165–175.

42 Nuthall, G. (2007). *The hidden lives of learners*. NZCER Press.

43 Bjork, R. A., & Bjork, E. L. (2020). Desirable difficulties in theory and practice. *Journal of Applied Research in Memory and Cognition*, 9(4), 475–479.

44 Murayama, K. (2023). Motivation resides only in our language, not in our mental processes. In M. Bong, J. Reeve & S. Kim (Eds.), *Motivation science: Controversies and insights* (pp. 65–75). Oxford University Press.

45 Niemivirta, M., Tapola, A., Tuominen, H., & Viljaranta, J. (2024). Developmental trajectories of school-beginners' ability self-concept, intrinsic value and performance in mathematics. *British Journal of Educational Psychology*, 94(2), 441–459.

46 van Bergen, E., Hart, S. A., Latvala, A., Vuoksimaa, E., Tolvanen, A., & Torppa, M. (2023) Literacy skills seem to fuel literacy enjoyment, rather than vice versa. *Developmental Science*, 26(3), e13325.

47 Deci, E. L., & Ryan, R. M. (1985). *Intrinsic motivation and self-determination in human behavior*. Plenum.

48 Garon-Carrier, G., et al. (2010). Intrinsic motivation and achievement in mathematics in elementary school: A longitudinal investigation of their association. *Child Development*, 87(1), 165–175.

49 Rosenshine, B. (2012). Principles of instruction: Research-based strategies that all teachers should know. *American Educator*, 36(1), 12–39.

50 Pólya, G. (1945). *How to solve it: A new aspect of mathematical method*. Princeton University Press.

51 Rousseau, J.-J. (1979). *Émile, or on education*. Translated by Allan Bloom. Basic Books.

52 Bardet, J.-P. (1987). La mortalité des enfants trouvés, aux XVIIe et XVIIIe siècles [The mortality rate of foundlings in the 17th and 18th centuries]. In R. Bouvier (Ed.), *Sur la population Française au XVIIIe et au XIXe siècles: Hommage à Marcel Reinhard* [On the French population in the 18th and 19th centuries: Homage to Marcel Reinhard] (pp. 79–96). Société de Démographie Historique,.

53 Voltaire. (1879). Le sentiment des citoyens (1764). In *Œuvres complètes de Voltaire* (Vol. 25, pp. 309–314). Garnier.

54 Coe, R. (2013). *Improving education: A triumph of hope over experience.* Inaugural lecture, Durham University, 18 June.

55 Hodson, D. (1985). Philosophy of science, science and science education. *Studies in Science Education*, 12(1), 25–57.

    Hodson, D. (1988). Experiments in science and science teaching. *Educational Philosophy and Theory*, 20(2), 53–66.

56 Kirschner, P. A. (2009). Epistemology or pedagogy, that is the question. In S. Tobias & T. M. Duffy (Eds.), *Constructivist instruction: Success or failure?* (pp. 144–157). Routledge/Taylor & Francis Group. Available at: https://lexiconic.net/pedagogy/epist.pdf

57 Chi, M. T. H., Feltovich, P. J., & Glaser, R. (1979). Categorization and representation of physics problems by experts and novices. *Cognitive Science*, 5(2), 121–152

    Chi, M. T. H., Glaser, R., & Rees, E. R (1982). Expertise in problem solving. In R. J. Sternberg (Ed.), *Advances in the psychology of human intelligence* (Vol. 1, pp. 1–75). Erlbaum.

58 De Groot, A. D. (1946). Het denken van den schaker. Een experimenteel-psychologische studie. [Thought and choice in chess: An experimental psychological study.] Noord-Hollandsche Uitgevers Maatschappij

    Chase, W. G., and Simon, H. A. (1973). Perception in chess. *Cognitive Psychology*, 4(1), 55–81.

59 See www.kirschnered.nl/2022/07/15/the-mind-as-a-natural-information-processing-system/

60 Kirschner, P. A., Sweller, J., & Clark, R. E. (2006). Why minimal guidance during instruction does not work: An analysis of the failure of constructivist, discovery, problem-based, experiential, and inquiry-based teaching. *Educational Psychologist*, 41(2), 75–86.

61 Kalyuga, S., Ayres, P., Chandler, P., & Sweller, J. (2003). The expertise reversal effect. *Educational Psychologist*, 38(1), 23–31.

62 Wiliam, D. (1999). Formative assessment in mathematics. Part 1: Rich questioning. *Equals: Mathematics and Special Educational Needs*, 5(2), 15–18.

63 In chapter 1 of *How Learning Happens* we tell the story of how Miller came up with the number, why telephone numbers have seven digits and how Cowan updated it.

64 Rosenshine, B. (2010). *Principles of instruction.* International Academy of Education, UNESCO. Geneva, Switzerland: International Bureau of Education.

65 Kirschner, P. A., Sweller, J., & Clark, R. E. (2006). Why minimal guidance during instruction does not work: An analysis of the failure of constructivist, discovery, problem-based, experiential, and inquiry-based teaching. *Educational Psychologist*, 41(2), 75–86.

66 Mayer, R. E. (2022). Cognitive theory of multimedia learning. In R. E. Mayer & L. Fiorella (Eds.), *The Cambridge handbook of multimedia learning* (3rd edn, pp. 57–72). Cambridge University Press.

67 Bjork, R. A. (1994). Memory and metamemory considerations in the training of human beings. In J. Metcalfe & A. Shimamura (Eds.), *Metacognition: Knowing about knowing* (pp. 185–205). MIT Press.

68 Britannica. (n.d.). *Clever Hans*. Encyclopaedia Britannica. www.britannica.com/topic/Clever-Hans

69 Soderstrom, N. C., & Bjork, R. A. (2015). Learning versus performance: An integrative review. *Perspectives on Psychological Science*, 10(2), 176–199.

70 Kirschner, P. A., Sweller, J., & Clark, R. E. (2006). Why minimal guidance during instruction does not work: An analysis of the failure of constructivist, discovery, problem-based, experiential, and inquiry-based teaching. *Educational Psychologist*, 41(2), 75–86.

71 In Memoriam A.H.H., an elegy written by Alfred, Lord Tennyson. A.H.H. stands for his friend Arthur Henry Hallum. The original is 'Tis better to have loved and lost than to never have loved at all'.

72 Craik, F. I. M., & Lockhart, R. S. (1972). Levels of processing: A framework for memory research. *Journal of Verbal Learning and Verbal Behavior*, 11(6), 671–684.

73 van Merriënboer, J. J. G., Kirschner, P. A., & Frèrejean, J. (2024). *Ten steps to complex learning*. Routledge.

74 Bjork, R. A. (1994). Memory and metamemory considerations in the training of human beings. In J. Metcalfe & A. Shimamura (Eds.), *Metacognition: Knowing about knowing* (pp. 185–205). MIT Press.

Bjork, R. A. (1994). Institutional impediments to effective training. In D. Druckman & R. A. Bjork (Eds.), *Learning, remembering, believing: Enhancing human performance* (pp. 295–306). National Academy Press.

75 Fiorella, L., & Mayer, R. E. (2015). *Learning as a generative activity: Eight learning strategies that promote understanding.* Cambridge University Press.

Fiorella, L., & Mayer, R. E. (2016). Eight ways to promote generative learning. *Educational Psychology Review, 28,* 717–741.

See also *How Learning Happens*, 2nd edition, chapter 14 and generative learning strategies in *How Teaching Happens,* chapter 13.

76 Bjork, E. L., & Bjork, R. A. (2011). Making things hard on yourself, but in a good way: Creating desirable difficulties to enhance learning. In M. A. Gernsbacher, R. W. Pew, L. M. Hough, & J. R. Pomerantz (Eds.), Psychology and the real world: Essays illustrating fundamental contributions to society (pp. 56–64). Worth Publishers.

77 Shaw, G. B. (n.d.). As quoted in Keane, M. (2011). *The quotable wisdom of G. B. Shaw: An encyclopaedia of quotes* (p. 47). Global Media Publications.

78 Oliver, T. (1986). *The real Coke, the real Story* (p. 178). Random House.

79 Cuban, L. (2013). *Inside the black box of classroom practice: Change without reform in American education.* Harvard Education Press.

80 Rance, G., Chisari, D., Saunders, K., & Rault, P. (2023). School classroom acoustics affect children's reading acquisition. *Journal of Educational Psychology,* 115(3), 477–490.

81 Mealings, K. T., Dillon, H., Buchholz, J. M., & Demuth, K. (2015). An assessment of open plan and enclosed classroom listening environments for young children: Part 1 – Children's questionnaires. *Journal of Educational, Pediatric & (Re)Habilitative Audiology,* 21, 1–17.

82 Azuma, K., Kagi, N., Yanagi, U., & Osawa, H. (2020). Effects of low-level inhalation exposure to carbon dioxide in indoor environments: A short review on human health and psychomotor performance. *Indoor Air,* 31(1), 16–25.

83 Cuban, L. (2004). The open classroom: Were schools without walls just another fad? *Education Next,* 4(2), 68–71.

84 National Reading Panel. (2000). *Teaching children to read: An evidence-based assessment of the scientific research literature on reading and its implications for reading instruction.* National Institute of Child Health and Human Development.

85 Gardner, H. (1983). *Frames of mind: The theory of multiple intelligences.* Basic Books.

86 Gardner, H. (1995). Reflections on multiple intelligences: Myths and messages. *Phi Delta Kappan, 77,* 200–209.

87 This is known as 'implementation fidelity' which is defined as whether an intervention or instructional method was actually carried out as designed or intended.

88 Elmore, R. F. (1996). Getting to scale with good educational practice. *Harvard Educational Review,* 66(1), 1–27.

89 Darling-Hammond, L., Hyler, M. E., & Gardner, M. (2017). *Effective teacher professional development.* Palo Alto, CA: Learning Policy Institute.

90 Schmidt, W. H., & Prawat, R. S. (2006). Curriculum coherence and national control of education: Issue or non-issue? *Journal of Curriculum Studies,* 38(6), 641–658.

91 Mayer, R. E. (2004). Should there be a three-strikes rule against pure discovery learning? *American Psychologist,* 59(1), 14–19.

92 Fixsen, D. L., Naoom, S. F., Blase, K. A., Friedman, R. M., & Wallace, F. (2005). *Implementation research: A synthesis of the literature.* Tampa, FL: University of South Florida, Louis de la Parte Florida Mental Health Institute, The National Implementation Research Network.

93 Willingham, D. T. (2012). Measured approach or magical elixir? How to tell good science from bad. *American Educator,* 36(3), 4–12.

94 James Randi in *An Honest Liar.* Weinstein, J., & Measom, T. (April 18, 2014). *An honest liar* [Film]. Flim Flam Films.

95 Randi, J. (1975). *The magic of Uri Geller.* Ballantine Books.

96 James Randi Educational Foundation
https://web.randi.org/
https://en.wikipedia.org/wiki/James_Randi_Educational_Foundation